LOS
ANGELES
# Dodgers
## PITCHERS

# LOS ANGELES
# Dodgers
## PITCHERS

*Seven Decades of Diamond Dominance*

## DON LECHMAN

THE
History
PRESS

Published by The History Press
Charleston, SC 29403
www.historypress.net

*Cover images*: Front: top three images courtesy of the Sporting News Archives; stadium image by Kwong Yee Cheng. Back: images, left to right, are courtesy of James Zar and the Los Angeles Dodgers; the Los Angeles Dodgers; and Tula Corning.

First published 2012

ISBN 978.1.540232113

Library of Congress CIP data applied for.

*Notice*: The information in this book is true and complete to the best of our knowledge. It is offered without guarantee on the part of the author or The History Press. The author and The History Press disclaim all liability in connection with the use of this book.

*This book is dedicated to my two grandchildren,*
*Kevin Jonathan Rodriguez and River Isabella Rodriguez,*
*who light up my life.*

# Contents

# Acknowledgements

My first tribute goes to my friend and editor Jerry Roberts of The History Press. His overseeing, assistance and dedication to this project made the book possible. I also want to thank my wife, Patricia Dee, who has put up with my endless hours of writing and cursing statistics and visiting baseball parks across the land, as well as my sporting obsessions, including baseball, my longtime love and affliction.

Thanks also go to Mark Langill, official historian of the Los Angeles Dodgers; Ian Allen of South Bay Baseball Cards Inc.; Michael Bernstein of Upper Deck; artist James Zar of San Pedro, California; Shawn Schrager of the Sporting News Archive in Charlotte, North Carolina; and Panini America, USA in Houston, Texas.

Also, this fan appreciates the contributions of one Vincent Edward Scully, longtime Dodger broadcaster, to the success of the Dodger pitching staff, as well as his being a great linchpin in my allegiance all of these years to the Dodgers. Scully is held in high regard by the Dodger faithful and practically everyone else: In 2009, he was named the best sportscaster of all time by the National Sportswriters and Sportscasters Association. If Vin said great things about any pitcher, they obviously were true. And he has said plenty. Vin, of course, started announcing the L.A. Dodger games after coming west with the team from Brooklyn.

He doesn't just seem like one of the family—he is family. His voice is soothing, unpretentious and undemanding but at the same time vibrant and full of life, in the house, the car, the stadium or wherever you may be.

His knowledge and nuances enlighten and entertain the listener. Nobody tells stories better than Scully, and nobody could possibly have more. Every inning of every game, he has something funny, dramatic or human to tell. His fairness is legendary. He calls the game the way he sees it and always lets the listener know where the home and the away players stand. He does not hesitate to reveal the faux pas by his own team. Here's one of his most famous calls, about that most famous Los Angeles Dodger pitcher's most famous game:

> *One and one to Harvey Kuenn. Now he's ready. Fastball, high, ball two. You can't blame a man for pushing just a little bit now. Sandy backs off, mops his forehead, runs his left index finger along his forehead, dries it off on his left pants leg. All the while Kuenn is just waiting. Now Sandy looks in. Into his windup and the two-one pitch to Kuenn: Swung on and missed, strike two. It is 9:46 p.m.*
>
> *Two and two to Harvey Kuenn, one strike away. Sandy into his windup, here's the pitch:*
>
> *Swung on and missed: A perfect game!* [Thirty-eight seconds of cheering by the crowd.]
>
> *On the scoreboard in right field it is 9:46 p.m. in the City of the Angels, Los Angeles, California. And a crowd of 29,139 just sitting in to see the only pitcher in baseball history to hurl four no-hit, no-run games. He has done it four straight years, and now he caps it: On his fourth no-hitter he made it a perfect game. And Sandy Koufax, whose name will always remind you of strikeouts, did it with a flurry. He struck out the last six consecutive batters. So when he wrote his name in capital letters in the record books, that "K" stands out even more than the O-U-F-A-X.*

That's vintage Scully, Los Angeles's national institution. Nobody could pitch a line like him.

# Introduction

A good pitcher is worth a dozen right fielders, unless one of them is Babe Ruth, Hank Aaron or Roberto Clemente. Pitching a baseball is an art, requiring mind, body and spirit. Stepping onto the pitcher's mound demands mettle and poise. Hanging in there inning after inning requires sheer guts. Dominating a game from the rubber time after time, year after year, requires a special kind of force of nature. As an athletic feat repeated dozens and dozens of times per game, pitching is ostensibly and hopefully honed toward perfection. And that is the elusive illusion: perfection will never be achieved.

To be perfect, one pitcher would have to strike out twenty-seven batters on eighty-one pitches. In golf, one would have to shoot an eighteen on an eighteen-hole course. In basketball, a player would need to make every basket and free throw, grab every rebound and prevent the other man from scoring. Sporting perfection is as elusive as any brand of perfection. Pitchers never stop trying to achieve perfection, and some of them have come close. The highest marks on a consistent, collective, team-wise basis have been achieved by one group of throwers over all others: the Los Angeles Dodgers.

Good pitchers have been held in very high regard by nearly everyone, with exceptions like Boston Red Sox Hall of Fame slugger Ted Williams, who thought they were the dumbest guys to walk the face of the earth. What he really meant is that he did not have any respect for someone who was not as well prepared to pitch as he was to hit.

Not very many Dodgers hurlers have approached pitching perfection. But some have thrown no-hitters, many of them have pitched valiantly in late innings and few were truly remarkable down the stretch, taking the club into the playoffs. And they have come closer than any other franchise's collective pitching staff to dominance of the sport. This book isolates the Dodgers' pitchers, explains their individual contributions, particularly on the World Series–winning teams of 1959, 1963, 1965, 1981 and 1988, the other World Series–participating clubs of 1966, 1974, 1977 and 1978 and the playoff contenders of 1983, 1985, 1995, 1996, 2004, 2006, 2008 and 2009.

No team except the New York Yankees has made as many playoff appearances since 1958 as the Los Angeles Dodgers. No team made it so far toward the ultimate World Series goal so many times by leaning on their pitching. The Dodgers have had more winners, nine, of the Cy Young Award—conferred annually on the league's best pitcher—than any other franchise: the overpowering Don Drysdale in 1962; great protean southpaw Sandy Koufax in 1963, 1965 and 1966; brilliant reliever Mike Marshall in 1974; Mexican-born "phenom" Fernando Valenzuela in 1981; breakthrough star Orel Hershiser in 1988; BB-throwing closer Eric Gagne in 2003; and new kid on the mound, Clayton Kershaw, in 2011. (Don Newcombe was also named winner of the Cy Young Award in 1956—for the Brooklyn Dodgers.)

In perhaps the most stunning statistic in the fifty-three years that the Dodgers have reigned in Los Angeles, the club has led the National League in team earned run average twenty times—nearly two-fifths of the greater half-century from 1958 through 2011—including half of the 1960s, most of the 1970s, four times in the 1980s and three times in the new century. No other team in major-league history comes close to posting such dominant hurling statistics.

Earned run average (ERA) has been the most telling stat in computing the value of pitchers throughout baseball history. A major-league pitcher is judged more on the basis of his earned run average than by his won-lost record or his propensity for strikeouts—although the L.A. Dodgers can boast plenty of pitchers who led the league or Major Leagues in those categories, too. The ERA represents the average number of earned runs given up by a pitcher per nine innings. An earned run is any run that the opponent scores off a particular pitcher except for runs scored as a result of errors or walks. If Don Drysdale, for instance, gave up two solo home runs in one game, and then an error caused another run to score, he is only credited with those first two runs that were "his fault."

It's instructive to briefly look back at the fortunes of the Brooklyn Dodgers before owner Walter O'Malley brought the club to Los Angeles for the 1958 season. The move out of Brooklyn has always been characterized as particularly heartbreaking and even heinous—a slap in the face to a loyal fan base who loved 'da Bums of Brooklyn as family members and who supported them ritualistically, watching them in the intimate confines of Ebbets Field. In sporting lore, the moving of the Dodgers from Brooklyn made the midnight exits in the National Football League (NFL) of the Baltimore Colts to Indianapolis and the Cleveland Browns to Baltimore (to become the Ravens) seem like happy-go-lucky skips along the Yellow Brick Road. O'Malley was reviled by the New York press and despised by thousands of New Yorkers for literally generations, even as he was embraced by the L.A. media and Southern California fans. The politics of defection aside, the Dodgers' move to L.A. proved to be a huge economic success and provided a great reinvigoration for the club.

The move from East Coast to West was motivated by economic issues and prodded by the great success, both team-wise and attendance-wise, of the move of the floundering Boston Braves to Milwaukee in 1953 and, later, when they represented the NL in the World Series of 1957 and 1958. O'Malley and his crosstown rival, Horace Stoneham, owner of the New York Giants, both knew that the upkeep of their stadiums was a responsibility and a drain on finances. The Polo Grounds, where the Giants played, needed as many upgrades as Ebbets Field. Both wanted to build new ballparks, and O'Malley was particularly annoyed by the politics and cost of building a new home somewhere within the confines of Brooklyn.

So, Stoneham and O'Malley moved away together, relocating in tandem for the 1958 campaign to the West Coast—the Giants to San Francisco and the Dodgers to L.A. Since then, the Dodgers consistently have been the leading team—or one of the leading teams—in attendance each year. Some years they drew more than 3 million people to Dodger Stadium, which has a seating capacity of 56,000 and can, in rare circumstances, squeeze in nearly 58,000. Ebbets Field had an original capacity of 23,000—later expanded to 34,000 and then adjusted to 32,000—and the most O'Malley ever drew to the slum-surrounded wooden ballpark in Flatbush was 1.8 million in 1947.

Most years, Ebbets Field attendance hovered around 1 million. The first year that the team played on the West Coast, in Los Angeles Memorial Coliseum, it drew 1.8 million, equaling the best annual attendance the team could muster in New York, or nearly 600,000 more people than in its final year, 1957, in Ebbets Field. The move to L.A. was the best thing the Dodgers ever did, economically.

Team-wise, the move was transcendent. Consider that in fifty-three years the L.A. Dodgers won five World Series in L.A., participated in nine and made the playoffs seventeen times. In the sixty-seven years between 1890, when the Brooklyn Dodgers became a member of the National League (NL), and their move to Los Angeles after the 1957 season, the club won one World Series, in 1955, and lost nine, most of those to the Yankees, as well as lost twice in the NL playoffs—to the St. Louis Cardinals in 1946 and to the Giants in 1951 via Bobby Thomson's historic home run. Compared to L.A.'s twenty team ERA titles in fifty-three years, Brooklyn accumulated nine seasons of the same sort of pitching dominance in sixty-seven seasons. As far as individual ERA titles, L.A. won nine (five by Koufax, from 1962 through 1966) and Brooklyn won four (three by Dazzy Vance).

The near perfect weather all season in Los Angeles and the nonpareil fan support in the friendly confines of Dodger Stadium, built for the 1962 season, have contributed to the team's perennial breeding of throwers outside the Snowbelt. Friendly is an understatement, since the Dodgers have passed more patrons through the turnstiles since 1958 than any other franchise in major American team sports.

Here, one theory claims, the night air in the stadium's neighborhood, Chavez Ravine, is heavy for some reason, which keeps balls in the park that might go out elsewhere. Sluggers have never thrived at Dodger Stadium, and only one Dodger has been a home run champion: Matt Kemp with 39 in 2011 (although Frank Howard, Jimmy Wynn and Pedro Guerrero flirted with the idea). So, merely as a survival measure in their home field, the reasoning goes, pitching would have to trump all else.

The phenomenal success of Sandy Koufax at Dodger Stadium was once expressed by the late, great Jim Murray, sports columnist for the *Los Angeles Times*, in terms of the lousy team hitting. "What makes Sandy Koufax so great is the same thing that made Walter Johnson great," Murray wrote, referencing the Hall of Fame pitcher for the Washington Senators. "The team behind him is the ghastliest scoring team in history. They pile up runs at the rate of one every nine innings. This is a little like making Rembrandt paint on the back of cigar boxes, giving Paderewski a piano with two octaves, Caruso singing with a high school chorus. With the Babe Ruth Yankees, Koufax would have been the first undefeated pitcher in history."

An urban legend of Chavez Ravine that has a basis in fact is that the team has always kept the infield grass high to help slow down hard-hit ground balls for the infielders to make plays on them, basically supporting a club that has been manifestly built around its pitching staff. Add to this the hard fact that the mound in Dodger Stadium was conveniently elevated for the team's power pitchers. In the early 1960s, "enforcement of the rulebook concerning the height of the mound was extremely lax, nonexistent really, and the Dodgers had built their mound way up in the air, giving maximum advantage to a power pitcher," wrote famed baseball historian Bill James. This allowed for tall power pitchers such as Don Drysdale and Stan Williams (and such similar opposition hurlers as Bob Gibson, Ferguson Jenkins and Bob Veale) the aspect of fireballing down on batters.

Outside of pitching, the other talents on which the Dodgers have put secondary premiums are the related aspects of speed and defense. When you don't have the offense to clout the ball, stretching for the extra base or stealing bases becomes a modus operandi. Maury Wills was only the most famous of the Dodger base pilferers, leading the NL in that category each year from 1960 through 1965. Junior Gilliam, Willie Davis, Davey Lopes, Pedro Guerrero, Delino DeShields and Rafael Furcal were others who consistently pushed themselves to take the extra base or steal one. These opportunists were the ones who often meant the difference as the hometown pitchers held off the opposition's bats—by scoring that needed run in the tradition of Dodger victories with scores such as 1–0, 2–1 and 3–2.

Likewise, in the field, the team has consistently been one of the top fielding clubs, using speed and quickness to cut off sharply hit grounders and line drives, vacuuming the infield and snatching screamers in the gaps in support of the pitchers (and their ERAs). Some pitchers helped themselves, as Andy Messersmith won Gold Gloves pitching in 1974 and 1975 for the Dodgers, and Fernando Valenzuela and Orel Hershiser also earned the coveted defensive honor. But being the best in the field was also a badge of honor, particularly at first base, where multiple Gold Gloves were earned by Dodgers Gil Hodges, Wes Parker and Steve Garvey.

As a fresh franchise on the West Coast, the Dodgers also lucked into a happy accident. The settling in L.A. coincided with the mercurial rises of lefty Sandy Koufax and right-hander Don Drysdale as two of the most overpowering pitchers the game had yet seen. That they blossomed so fully, and became superior major league stars simultaneously on the same staff, leading the club to four World Series in eight years and winning three of them, ingrained in Dodger management the value and winning power of great pitching. From those World Championships forward, the franchise put an emphasis on drafting, trading for and acquiring in any way possible the best throwers available. This is why the club ended up with more quality pitchers over the long haul than other teams.

This perennial reinforcement of the team's great strength also has something to do with the fact that no career Dodger pitcher has won 300 games in the time-honored manner of such great, late twentieth-century hurlers as Greg Maddux (355), Roger Clemens (354), Steve Carlton (329) and Nolan Ryan (324). New blood has been consistently infused into the Dodger staff. And, of course, in the era of free agency, many of the bright stars found greener pastures elsewhere. Don Sutton finished with 324 victories, but "only" 233 of them came in a Dodger uniform. The lack of career wins for Dodger icons is mostly due to poor offense. Even when the pitchers managed to throw tough and hard, the batters couldn't give them enough runs to win. Ten career starters—Sandy Koufax, Don Drysdale, Fernando Valenzuela, Clayton Kershaw, Tommy John, Kevin Brown, Andy Messersmith, Tim Belcher, Alejandro Pena and Guillermo Mota—posted career ERAs of under 3.00, or less than three runs per game. Likewise, nine major relievers—Jim Brewer, Ron Perranoski, Jay Howell, Tom Niedenfurer, Takashi Saito, Steve Howe, Phil Regan, Jim Gott and Scott Radinksy—had ERAs of under 3.00.

As this legacy of premium pitching went to press, good news came to the Dodger faithful in 2012 when the team divested itself of the millstone around its neck, owner Frank McCourt. The Boston Irishman, obviously no dummy, sold the team for $2.15 billion, or five times more than he paid ($430 million) for it. He sold it to a group of investors led by one of Los Angeles's greatest heroes (on and off the court): Earvin "Magic" Johnson, former star point guard of the NBA's Los Angeles Lakers.

This book is a general history that covers the Dodgers' fortunes in terms of that pitching. The front portion of the book is a general year-by-year history of the Dodgers, with the emphasis on their pitching staff. The second part ranks the team's pitchers and also puts them in perspective with other contemporaries in the league. Special attention is paid to Sanford Braun Koufax, perhaps the greatest southpaw that the game has ever seen, and the phenomenon of "Fernandomania," which swept the baseball world in the early 1980s when Mexican son Fernando Valenzuela became one of baseball's most unhittable hurlers. Other "hill aces" covered include Johnny Podres, Clem Labine, Roger Craig, Stan Williams, Larry Sherry, Ron Perranoski, Bob Miller, Phil Regan, Tommy John, Al Downing, Andy Messersmith, Burt Hooten, Alejandro Pena, Ramon Martinez, Kevin Gross, Tim Worrell, Eric Gagne, Clay Kershaw and many, many more. The back of the book carries charts on various baseball stats: wins, losses, earned run average, win percentage, strikeouts, bases on balls, fewest hits per nine innings, fewest home runs given up and so on.

The purpose of this book is to give the true baseball fan, that diehard lover of statistics and extra-inning games, a detailed look at the greatest pitchers who ever played for the blue and white, as well as a little glimpse at all the "also-pitched guys" for the Dodgers. A true Dodger fan might be surprised at some of the forgotten hurlers who passed through the Dodger bullpen, going and coming from somewhere else, often the minor leagues.

The book is also a tribute to all of these pitchers, a nostalgic look at some of the guys, who, like Manager Tommy Lasorda, bled blue, if only for a year or two. If a pitcher has passed on to that bullpen in the sky, that will be indicated.

# The 1950s

The 1950s was the greatest decade in Dodger history on either coast, straddling as it did both the Brooklyn and Los Angeles eras. Not only did the Bums win the National League pennant fully half the time— in 1952, 1953, 1955, 1956 and 1959—they also finally won the World Series in 1955 over their archrivals, the New York Yankees. And they won it all again in 1959 over the Chicago White Sox in just their second year in Los Angeles. The Dodgers of the 1950s—managed by Burt Shotton in 1950, Chuck Dressen from 1951 to 1953 and Walter Alston from 1954 through the end of the decade—were certainly one of the greatest baseball dynasties in major-league history. They shared that status, at the time and in retrospect, with their crosstown rivals, the Yankees. The Dodgers team of the next decade won more games—875 in the 1960s, compared to 833 in the 1950s—but teams played more games as well, as the majors went to a 162-game season in 1962 from the 154-game annuals played since 1904.

It's instructive to the discussion of the great worth of the Los Angeles pitchers to objectively select an all-time Dodgers team going back to 1950. My position picks for that team would be Roy Campanella (catcher), Gil Hodges (first base), Jackie Robinson (second), Ron Cey (third), Pee Wee Reese (shortstop), Tommy Davis (left field), Duke Snider (center) and Carl Furillo (right). Six of these eight everyday players are from the Brooklyn era, with four of them (Campanella, Reese, Robinson and Snider) enshrined in the Baseball Hall of Fame, and Hodges probably should be. If arguments were to prevail for the selection of Maury Wills over Reese at shortstop, *most of the lineup* would still be guys who played most of their careers in Ebbets Field.

The Dodgers simply could not find that many consistently solid keepers on offense and in the field through the Los Angeles years. It's phenomenal to think that this sake-of-argument team, which played eight years in Brooklyn and fifty-three in L.A., would still be dominated at the extra-pitching positions by the players of the Brooklyn era. On the West Coast, the Dodgers' position players were often a patchwork cobbled together around a star or two, always dependent on the guys who climbed the hill and hurled the ball.

To complete this prefabricated argument, the all-time pitching staff of ten for the same time period would consist of Sandy Koufax, Don Drysdale, Fernando Valenzuela, Orel Hershiser, Claude Osteen, Don Sutton, Don Newcombe and Carl Erskine, with relievers Eric Gagne, and Jim Brewer. (Clayton Kershaw could almost make this list after only a few seasons.) Note that eight of ten pitchers are from the L.A. era, with Newcombe and Erskine the only ones to have played most of their careers in Brooklyn. Both played a year or two for the Dodgers in Los Angeles but were soon out of baseball. Koufax and Drysdale started in Brooklyn but led the charge in establishing the Dodgers and their pitching superiority in the City of Angels. The greater number of outstanding pitchers arrived after the Brooklyn era.

The Dodgers' move to Los Angeles initiated a rush to Southern California by sports franchises noticing the 1.8 million Angelenos in 1958 attending the Dodgers games at the Los Angeles Memorial Coliseum, an oval created for the 1932 Olympic Games in L.A. and much more suited to football than baseball. The NFL's Los Angeles Rams were already in operation, but the arrival of the then more popular national sport of baseball, with one of its most popular teams, the great Dodgers, paved the way for other franchises to test the suitability of L.A. as a major sports center: the National Basketball Association's Los Angeles Lakers' arrival in 1960 from Minneapolis, the maiden season of the American Football League's Los Angeles Chargers the same year (even though they jumped down the coast to San Diego the following year) and the American League's expansion Los Angeles Angels in 1961. Tangentially, television, an increasingly important industry that was becoming more significant to sports, moved practically en masse from New York to L.A. over the same few years to symbiotically camp out near, and then share the wealth with, its big brother, the movie industry.

Dodgers owner Walter O'Malley's move of the Dodgers was a watershed moment for baseball and big-time sports. Before his influence encouraged Horace Stoneham of the Giants to move with the Dodgers to the West Coast, the Major Leagues were composed of sixteen teams in ten cities, none farther west than Missouri and only two, Baltimore and Washington, D.C., a few miles south of the Mason-Dixon line. Sportswriter Roger Kahn very succinctly described in retrospect the impact of the Dodgers' move on professional sports: "Walter O'Malley nationalized the big leagues."

Don Drysdale pitched the very first L.A. game before 78,672 people, beating the new San Francisco Giants, 6–5. All the pitchers were concerned about playing in a football stadium, the Coliseum, with its 250-foot left-field foul line. To prevent many of the routine fly balls from becoming home runs, the Dodgers erected two 40-foot-high steel poles and put up a screen 140 feet long. *Sports Illustrated* remarked that the odd, makeshift monster resembled the Brooklyn Bridge. "It's nothing but a sideshow," Drysdale said of the Coliseum. "Who feels like playing baseball in this place?"

The oblong shape of the field just wasn't made for baseball. "They had room at the L.A. Coliseum for 93,000 people and two outfielders," sportscaster Lindsey Nelson once cracked. In 1958, 182 homers were hit to left field in the Coliseum, 3 to center and 8 over the right-field wall. The Coliseum especially took away home runs from Duke Snider. A left-handed hitter, the Silver Fox had led the NL in homers in 1956 with 43 and in 1957 with 40. Clouting balls out into the vast expanse of right field in the Coliseum—440 feet away in right-center—Snider managed only 15 home runs in 1958. Willie Mays saw that coming. The first time the Giants were in town, Mays told Snider, according to the latter, "Duke, they killed you. Man, they took the bat right out of your hands."

Despite the attendance and the popularity of the team, especially with the Hollywood crowd, many of whom became lifelong fans, the Dodgers posted a lousy first year in one of the Major Leagues' most oddball stadiums of all time. The Dodgers won only 71 games (the same as 2005) to tie for the second-lowest number of wins in the team's history in California. The 63 wins in 1992 represented the lowest amount.

Part of the problem was the players' adjustment to Los Angeles itself. The West Coast sprawl wasn't the kind of neighborhood that Brooklyn had been to the Bums. Many of them still kept their homes in New York. "All of the veteran Dodgers who had become so accustomed to Brooklyn were at sea in Southern California," Drysdale reported in his autobiography, *Once a Bum, Always a Dodger*, written with Bob Verdi. "Guys like Gil [Hodges] had their families rooted in Brooklyn and they stayed there until summer, when school was out, and the kids would come west. He wound up living for a spell downtown."

Another reason for the Dodger downfall was the sudden and forever absence of the great Roy Campanella behind the plate and in the clubhouse. The catcher had been as integral a Brooklyn Dodger as practically anyone on the club. He was a three-time NL Most Valuable Player (in 1951, 1953 and 1955), a great defensive player, a solid batsman and an adroit handler of the pitching staff. He also was a pioneer in the sports race relations business as a teammate at Jackie Robinson's side. But "Campy's" great career came to a halt on the night of January 28, 1958, when the car he was driving overturned on a Long Island highway. He was paralyzed permanently from the shoulders down.

# 1958

Despite the strange new city, the still stranger stadium and the loss of one of baseball's greatest catchers, the Dodgers' pitching staff in 1958 still had its solid performers in Johnny Podres, who led the staff with 13 wins, followed by Drysdale with 12 and Sandy Koufax with 11. Koufax was twenty-two that year and had not yet discovered that he was destined to become one of the game's greatest pitchers. Drysdale was twenty-one, and Podres was the old man at twenty-five. Stan Williams posted a 9-7 record, with Clem Labine and Fred Kipp both 6-6, Carl Erskine 4-4, Johnny Klippstein 3-5, Roger Craig 2-1, Danny McDevitt 2-6, Don Bessent 1-0 and Bob Giallombardo and Ralph Mauriello both 1-1.

Two fan favorites in Brooklyn said goodbye to the team in the initial L.A. years. The former ace Don Newcombe, who had been a three-time 20-game winner in Brooklyn, posting a 27-6 mark to win the 1956 Cy Young Award, was one of the old guard who never made the full transition to Los Angeles. Newcombe went 0-6 before being traded to the Cincinnati Reds at midseason. He retired after a few more years, having matriculated to the Cleveland Indians. The other ace of bygone Brooklyn days (20-6 in 1953), Erskine, followed his .500 mark in 1958 with a 0-3 record in 1959, when he retired. A native of Anderson, Indiana, the state in which he still resides as of this writing, Erskine threw two no-hitters for the Bums and won 118 games in Brooklyn over ten years.

The 71 victories in 1958 registered as pathetic by the Dodgers' standards of the decade. The club finished 2 games ahead of the cellar-dwelling Philadelphia Phillies and 21 behind the pennant-winning Milwaukee Braves. The enduring Johnny Podres was a bright spot, posting the best ERA, 3.17, of the team's pitchers who threw more than one hundred innings. The team ERA was 4.47 and not the worst ever.

Fred Kipp, who was born in Piqua, Kansas, pitched four years in the majors. His best season by far was his .500 posting in 1958. Johnny Klippstein, a Washington, D.C., son, stayed through 1959, won 7 games for the Dodgers and was traded. The most games he ever won in a season was 12 in 1956, with Cincinnati, but he managed to hang on for eighteen years in the Major Leagues. Klippstein was among that breed of pitcher who brought a veteran savvy to any staff and, as a spot starter or middle reliever or other role player, managed to hang on in baseball for nearly two decades. He died in 2003 at the age of seventy-five.

Bessent, signed by the Yankees out of high school in Florida, was called up to the "show" in 1955 and posted a superb 8-1 rookie year. In 1956, he went 4-3, but with an ERA of 2.50. After that, he developed arm trouble and left the majors in 1958 after winning a game with the Dodgers. He spent several unsuccessful years in the minors before retiring in 1962. He became a salesman and died in 1990.

McDevitt was a left-hander from New York City who won 12 games for the Dodgers from 1958 through 1960. His best year was 1959, when he won 10 games and helped the Dodgers win the pennant. He died in Georgia in 2010 at age seventy-eight. Ralph Mauriello and Bob Giallombardo, both natives of Brooklyn, only pitched one year in the majors, 1958, and both finished 1-1. Nice stuff to tell their grandchildren.

The best thing that can be said about the Dodgers' meager fortunes in 1958 is that they set the stage for practically nowhere to go but up. How far up they managed to go is still kind of a shocker more than half a century later.

# 1959

"How can a team finish seventh one year and be World Champions the next?" was the rhetorical question posed by the flesh-and-blood namesake of *Koufax*, a 1966 autobiography coauthored with Ed Linn. "I'm not sure," he answered. "A team like the Dodgers…always feels that things are going to straighten out tomorrow…Athletes are like politicians; you have to feel in your bones that you're a winner or you wouldn't be in this business to start with…We were really not as bad as we had looked in the Lost Year in Los Angeles. It took us a year to accommodate ourselves to the Coliseum."

Accommodate? They got downright comfy. And they got some help. They picked up Wally Moon from the St. Louis Cardinals, and he became an all-star in the Coliseum. A left-handed hitter like Snider, Moon adapted to the park by learning to slice at pitches to send home runs high over the giant screen down the short foul line in left. These long pop-ups became known as "Moon Shots."

The pitching staff became known as one of the meanest to roam the Major Leagues. Down through the history of the Los Angeles Dodgers, and right from the start, the staff was armed, so to speak, by a coterie of driller killers. Don Drysdale was only the most famous. Simply by being Don Drysdale—one of the top power pitchers in the league and an extra-large presence on the mound at six feet, six inches and 220 pounds—he frightened batters off the plate and then perhaps would singe a few eyebrows with high inside hummers or test the bailing quickness of a batter with a potential rib tickler.

It was anyone's guess how far this reputation for mowing down opponents (especially as retaliation for Dodgers batters getting beaned) went as a reflection in the stats and win columns. But it was a fact of life that you could get hurt if you faced Los Angeles pitching. This condition was at its worst when Stan Williams took the hill. Another staff pitcher explained it. "People said me and Don Drysdale were mean, but Stan had it down to a science," said Larry Sherry, who threw for the blue from 1958 to 1963. "He actually kept a book inside his locker. It listed the guys he was gonna hit and *where* he was gonna hit them. Stan was also big. So none of the batters really wanted to fight him. Plus, they knew if there was a fight, he'd hit the next six batters in a row."

Williams, who was six feet, five inches and 240 pounds, threw for the Dodgers from 1958 to 1962 and spent a journeyman's later career with five different teams. The *Los Angeles Times*, no less, labeled Williams "the meanest pitcher of his time." Years later, he told journalist Steve Delsohn, "Well, the game was played differently then. It was a knockdown era. You tried every possible way to get a batter out. If nothing you tried worked, you drilled him in the ribs and started all over again." Williams also remembered his early training. "When I was a teenager, I had a coach who told me, 'Knock your grandmother on her ass if she has a bat in her hands.' That was pretty much my attitude," he said.

Koufax channeled his aggressiveness into throwing strikes. He started to find himself in mid-June 1959, when he pitched three complete games in a row for the first time in his life. The mercurial flashes of brilliance that would come to characterize his remarkable performances in the 1960s were seen in fits and starts. On August 31, against the Giants of Mays, McCovey and Cepeda in the Coliseum, Koufax broke Dizzy Dean's NL record and tied Bob Feller's major-league mark of eighteen strikeouts in a game.

Some of that old Brooklyn offensive support lingered on as the Dodgers hit 148 home runs, with Gil Hodges and Duke Snider clouting more than 20 and Wally Moon and Charlie Neal ending the season with 19 each. Curiously, Moon and Neal also shared the same number of triples, 11 apiece, to co-lead the NL. The Duke hit .308 with 23 home runs and 88 RBIs, and Moon also became one of the relatively rare L.A. Dodger .300 hitters at .302. The team batted .257, and the staff had a collective ERA of 3.79.

Drysdale led the team with 17 wins, followed by Podres with 14, Roger Craig with 11, Danny McDevitt with 10 and Koufax with 8. Larry Sherry won 7 games (and had an ERA of 2.19), with Stan Williams and Clem Labine both 5, Johnny Klippstein 4, Art Fowler and Chuck Churn both 3 and Gene Snyder 1. Fowler, from Converse, South Carolina, won 54 games in nine seasons—51 with other teams—and died in 2007 at age eighty-four. Churn, from Bridgetown, Virginia, spent three years in the majors, with his only victories being his last year with the Dodgers. Snyder, who was born in York, Pennsylvania, and died in 1996, played this one season in the bigs, when he won a game for the Dodgers.

A paltry 88 victories paced the National League that year, posted by both the Dodgers and the Milwaukee Braves. In a best-of-three playoff, L.A. swept the Braves, with Hodges scoring the winning run in the twelfth inning of Game 2 from second base on a grounder by Carl Furillo that Braves infielder Felix Mantilla threw wide of first base. The World Series was against the mighty Chicago White Sox, who won 94 games in the American League. The Sox hit .250 on the season, with Nelson Fox the top batter. The Sox's collective ERA was 3.29, and the staff ace, Early Wynn, paced the majors in wins with 22.

After losing to the Sox, 11–0, in the first game, the Dodgers won the next three and pulled out the series victory on a 9–3 win in the sixth game at Comiskey Park. The key to the Dodgers' success was, of course, pitching, but specifically the superb throwing of Larry Sherry. He pitched 12 $2/3$ innings across the four victories in the series, all in relief, winning 2 games and saving the other 2 for Drysdale and Podres. The cliché of "last man standing" was a heroic reality for Sherry in each Dodger win in the series, as he completed each of the 4 wins. He was simply masterly, bringing his best stuff when it counted the most and posting an astounding World Series ERA of 0.71.

Larry was the brother of Dodgers backup catcher Norm Sherry, who played from 1959 through 1963, including a year with the New York Mets. Larry Sherry had been born with clubfeet and required surgery as an infant. He was fitted with special shoes as a child. He defied the odds and excelled as an athlete at Fairfax High School in L.A. Sherry said that it was a great thrill to play with his brother on the same team and that it was something that the two had talked about as kids on sandlots around Los Angeles. They got their wish. Distinctions being what they are, it's worth mentioning that, with the Dodgers, Larry and Norm formed the first Jewish brothers battery in major-league history.

Sherry pitched four years on the Detroit Tigers staff and also spent time with the Houston Astros and California Angels. He retired in 1968 with a 53-44 record over eleven years and later coached for the Pittsburgh Pirates and the Angels. He died of cancer in 2006 at his home in Mission Viejo, California. Larry Sherry was voted the Most Valuable Player in the 1959 series—as if there were any other choice. His consistently superlative innings against the White Sox certainly rank him as one of the greatest World Series heroes of all time.

Gil Hodges led the series hitters with a .381 average, and second baseman Charlie Neal hit .370 with two homers. No one else on the Dodgers did much, but the White Sox did less. Game 5 drew 92,271 fans into the Coliseum, which is still a record not likely to be broken, since no stadium exceeds a capacity of 70,000.

Baseball historian Bill James claimed in 1997 that the 1959 Dodgers were "the weakest World Championship team of all time." In hindsight, perhaps. But nothing mitigates moving pains, Brooklyn sour grapes and the goofiness of the stadium like winning it all. A World Championship is a World Championship.

# The 1960s

The Dodgers in the 1960s reinforced the notion in Los Angeles, Brooklyn and everywhere in between that they were one of the best teams in baseball and one of the ruling franchises of big-time sports. It was a monumental decade for them, as they won the World Series in 1963 and 1965 and captured three pennants in all. The promise of the tandem of Sandy Koufax and Don Drysdale was fulfilled more sublimely than owner Walter O'Malley or Manager Walter Alston or anyone else may have imagined. The Dodgers' pitchers collected four Cy Young Awards: Drysdale in 1962 and Koufax in 1963, 1965 and 1966. The team boasted seven 20-game winners in that period—Koufax in 1963 (25-5), 1965 (23-12) and 1966 (27-9); Drysdale in 1962 (25-9) and 1965 (23-12); and, in 1969, Claude Osteen (20-11) and Bill Singer (20-12).

The only reason that the Dodgers pitching staff of the 1960s was not under a 3.00 earned run average for the decade was due to some slippage in 1961. The 4.04 ERA that season brought the whole team average up over 3.00. Still, the 1960s formed the best decade in Los Angeles Dodgers history for pitchers as they collectively posted a 3.12 ERA. Koufax's ERA was 2.64, Drysdale's 2.80, Osteen's 2.91, Singer's 2.59 and Don Sutton's 3.29. As far as relief pitchers, Jim Brewer posted a 2.62 ERA and Ron Perranowski a 2.56. No other team was close to this sort of run management of their opposing teams.

The Dodgers led the league in ERA and strikeouts five times each in the decade. Most of the time, the team was in the top four in complete games, and it was first in 1965 (58) and 1966 (52). As in most of the history of baseball, the 1960s was an era when the finishing of a game by a starting pitcher was not only a badge of honor but also something expected by management, teammates and the fans. A complete game was an indicator of success—of control, game management, dominance and winning.

The team moved into a new home in 1962—Dodger Stadium, built by O'Malley in a section of downtown Los Angeles known as Chavez Ravine—and it continued to be the most popular draw in American team sports. Before the phrase "state of the art" came into the language, Dodger Stadium became the jewel of baseball. Outfitted with all the amenities, attended by the Hollywood's royalty as well as the hoi polloi and inhabited by the extremely successful and popular Dodgers, the fifty-six-thousand-seat Dodger Stadium became an entertainment mecca for tourists as well as locals.

There are many names ensconced in Dodger lore from the 1960s for alliteration, ignominy and/or glory: Rip Repulski, Doug Camilli, Don Demeter, Joe Pignatano, Chuck Essegian, Bob Lillis, Bob Aspromonte, Larry Burright, Lee Walls, Ken McMullen, Dick Tracewski, Nate Oliver, Al Ferrara, Darryl Spencer, Jeff Torborg, John Kennedy, Lou Johnson and Dick Schofield. One of the great Dodger killers of all time, Stan "The Man" Musial, finished his lustrous career in 1963. Carl Furillo, Gil Hodges and Duke Snider—all Dodger greats from Brooklyn—hung up their spikes in the early 1960s. The most shocking thing was the retiring of Sandy Koufax at the end of 1966, the season of his most victories, 27.

"You go back to Babe Ruth before you get the idea of what Sandy Koufax meant to the grand old game," columnist Jim Murray wrote in the *Los Angeles Times*. "You go back to Joan of Arc before you get a model for the kids. Baseball lost more than a southpaw. Baseball lost a symbol. Baseball lost part of its integrity…There was no more thrilling sight in baseball than the first Koufax fastball. I always likened it in my mind to the first hard right Joe Louis threw in a fight."

Edward Gruver wrote in *Koufax*: "He left at high noon, a Hamlet in mid-soliloquy."

"I was at a banquet the night before the game when word spread that Koufax had retired," sportswriter George Sullivan remembered. "Nobody could believe it. It was like Pearl Harbor, one of those times when you remember exactly where you were and what you were doing."

STREET and SMITH'S OFFICIAL Yearbook

*1966* *Baseball*

50 CENTS

SANDY KOUFAX
L.A. Dodgers

Complete!
Up-to-date!
CLUB ROSTERS
SCHEDULES
AVERAGES
SLUGGING AVERAGES
NATIONAL LEAGUE
By ED PRELL
AMERICAN LEAGUE
By TIL FERDENZI
MINOR LEAGUES
By EDDIE FISHER
Out Of A Jam
With DP's
By MEL STOTTLEMYRE
N.Y. Yankees
Ouch!
By FRANK FINCH
Triple Thrills
By KEN SMITH
Power Plus
Speed
By BOB ADDIE
About Homers
By ROSCOE McGOWEN
FLEET FEET
TOUGH 400 TB
PLAYER'S TARGETS
NO-HITTERS
BB COMMISSIONERS
SERIES RECAP

Despite pitching in pain the entire 1966 season, Sandy Koufax hurled 323 innings with a 27-9 record and an ERA of 1.73, winning his third Cy Young Award in four years. He was runner-up for league MVP to Roberto Clemente. *Courtesy of the Sporting News Archives.*

Don Drysdale also had his two most magnificent seasons in the decade, winning 25 in 1962 and 23 in 1965. In 1969, he also retired at a young age, thirty-two, following some injuries.

"With all due respect to Don Larsen's perfect game, Don Drysdale pitched the two best World Series games I ever saw," Jim Murray wrote in 1969. "He beat the Yankees in one 1–0 (1963); he lost to Baltimore in the other, 1–0 (1966). That's the way these Dodger hitters were. You hit this Drysdale in self defense. You hit the ball or it hit you. Batters used to believe that Don put something on the ball that belonged on the scalp; that he was really Don 'Wetsdale.' But what was on a Drysdale pitch was venom."

Drysdale terrorized batsman. "If they knocked one of our guys down," he wrote, "I'd knock down two of theirs. If they knocked two of our guys down, I'd get four. You have to protect your hitters."

Johnny Podres played nine years in Los Angeles, from 1958 to 1966. The part that Podres played in the team's success in the early 1960s is often overlooked because of the greatness of Koufax and Drysdale. But Podres won 68 games in seven years in the decade, including 1961 when he was 18-5 and led the National League with a .783 winning percentage. "Johnny was a terrific clutch performer," Drysdale said, an "off the field a free spirit who could cure another guy's bad mood in two minutes…A flake? No just loose."

The Dodgers' greatest deal concerning pitchers in the 1960s came when they acquired left-hander Claude Osteen in a seven-player deal that sent Frank "Hondo" Howard and Pete Richert in December 1964 to the Washington Senators. Claude, who went on to win 147 games for the Dodgers, was a good batsman, accumulating more than 200 hits. "I loved hitting," Claude said once. "I thought of myself as a good hitter. I took pride in it and worked on hitting a lot." He hit nearly .200 with 76 RBIs and seven home runs.

Osteen's greatest moments were in the World Series when he shut out the Minnesota Twins, 4–0, in Game 3 in 1965. He also pitched brilliantly in Game 3 against the Baltimore Orioles in 1966, allowing three hits in seven innings, but eventually losing, 1–0. His final tally for the World Series was an ERA of 0.86, with seven strikeouts in twenty-one innings. "Osteen was a deliberate and poised pitcher, and he said he noticed substantial differences in the way modern pitchers throw," wrote Gregory Wolf for the Society of American Baseball Research. Osteen emphasized his control and ongoing in-game analysis. "The way scouts scout today, it is a possibility that guys like Tom Glavine, Randy Jones, myself, Tommy John might not have gotten signed today because [the scouts] are looking for 92–93-mile-an-hour pitches." Wolf contemplated this, saying, "That's a troubling thought as baseball would have been robbed of excellent pitchers. A thinking man's pitcher with an eye for detail, Claude Osteen should be remembered for his consistency, dependability, and professionalism."

The Dodgers seemed to always muster enough runs to just squeak by and win in the 1960s, with two players usually figuring in their offensive success. Leftfielder Tommy Davis won back-to-back NL batting titles with a .346 percentage (and 230 hits and 153 RBIs) in 1962 and .326 in 1963. Maury Wills made his mark stealing his record 104 bases in 1962 at the age of twenty-nine. Maury loved to run on certain pitchers—Curt Simmons, for instance, who threw for the Cardinals and Cubs in the 1960s after fourteen years with the Phillies. Wills hated to run against Milwaukee Braves ace Warren Spahn. "Whenever I was picked off by the pitcher, I knew that I had to come back the next time around with even more daring and aggressiveness," Maury wrote in *How to Steal a Pennant*. "It was important that the next time I got on base, I try to steal immediately. It became a challenge, and it was also necessary for me to condition the pitchers to respect me."

# 1960

The post–World Series jinx arrived in 1960 as the Dodgers won only 82 games, settling for fourth place in the eight-team National League, 13 games behind the eventual World Champion Pittsburgh Pirates. Drysdale won 15 games that year, followed by Podres, Stan Williams and Sherry, all with 14 victories. Koufax, Craig and Roebuck each won 8 games. Ed Palmquist, a native of Los Angeles, pitched two years for the Dodgers, going 47.2 innings with two losses. He died in 2010 in Santa Maria. Ed Rakow, who hailed from Pittsburgh, pitched one year for the Dodgers, ended up going 36-47 in the majors with four different teams. He died in 2000 in Florida. Jim Golden, who was born in Missouri, pitched two years for the Dodgers, going 2-1. The hitting was unremarkable, but Norm Larker batted .323 in 133 games.

# 1961

The Dodgers won 89 games in 1961 when Koufax discovered his true fireballing self. Both he and Johnny Podres won 18 games apiece. Williams won 15 and Drysdale 13. The great Ron Perranoski made his debut going 7-5 with an ERA of 2.51. Dick "Turk" Farrell, a native of Boston, showed up after a trade with Philadelphia and won 6 games; he left just as quickly after the season, in the expansion draft to Houston. In thirteen seasons elsewhere in the bigs, he won 100 games. Turk was killed in 1977 at age forty-three in an auto accident in England. Phil Ortega pitched five years for the Dodgers, going 0-2 in 1961 and 1962, but he won 7 games in 1964. Maury Wills led the offense with 173 hits and 35 stolen bases, and Wally Moon hit .328.

# 1962

The year 1962 was an impressive one for the Dodgers—for a while. Sandy Koufax pitched his first no-hitter on June 30 against the expansion New York Mets, winning 5–0. Unfortunately, he came down with a mysterious ailment (which later disappeared just as mysteriously) and had to stop pitching on July 14 for the rest of the season. He had already won 14 games. It was too bad, because with Maury Wills stealing 104 bases, the Dodgers had a great year, but they faltered down the stretch, losing a three-game set to St. Louis, allowing the rival Giants to tie them, forcing the fourth playoff in NL history.

Manager Smokey Alston asked Koufax if he would start the first game of the best-of-three playoff series because Drysdale and Podres had only two days' rest. Sandy agreed, but he had not pitched for two months due to his finger ailment. The Giants blew out the Dodgers in that first game, 8–0, as Billy Pierce pitched a three-hit shutout. The Dodgers came back to win the second game at Dodger Stadium, 8–7, in what was then the longest nine-inning game in major-league history at four hours and twenty-seven minutes.

The Giants went ahead 5–0 to really put a damper on the Dodger season, but L.A. came back with 7 runs in the bottom of the sixth inning.

BIG-D

IT HAS NEVER HAPPENED BEFORE
SIX STRAIGHT SHUTOUTS
FOR BIG-D

Don Drysdale won 187 games for the Dodgers in Los Angeles, including 25 in 1962, when he won the Cy Young Award, and 23 in 1965. Drysdale and Sandy Koufax formed one of the greatest pitching duos in baseball history. *Courtesy of the Los Angeles Dodgers and James Zar.*

Jim Gilliam walked, Duke Snider doubled, Tommy Davis hit a sacrifice fly, Wally Moon walked, Frank Howard singled, Doug Camilli singled, Andy Carey was hit by a pitch and Lee Walls hit a double to empty the bases and give the Dodgers a 6–5 lead. Walls later scored on Maury Wills's grounder, making the game 7–5. The Giants tied the score in the eighth inning, and the Dodgers won the game in the bottom of the ninth when Ron Fairly hit a walk-off sacrifice fly.

The joy was short-lived, however. In the final game, the Dodgers went into the top of the ninth at Dodger Stadium leading 4–2. The Giants' Matty Alou singled off of Ed Roebuck to lead off the inning. Willie McCovey and Felipe Alou walked. Willie Mays hit a single and moved to second on a wild pitch to Ed Bailey. Alston called on Stan Williams to relieve Roebuck. Williams intentionally walked Bailey to reload the bases and then walked Jim Davenport to give the Giants a 5–4 lead. They added to it as Jose Pagán reached first on an error, allowing Mays to score and extend the lead to 6–4.

Billy Pierce pitched a perfect bottom of the ninth to end the game, earning his only save of the season. And the Dodgers were history.

Podres and Williams both won 14 games in 1962 to lead the Dodgers. Roebuck had 10 wins, while Sherry went 7-3. Perranoski recorded 20 saves. Also lending credibility were Joe Moeller at 6-5 and Pete Richert at 5-4. Richert, who was born in Floral Park, New York, pitched thirteen seasons in the bigs, winning 80 games, and five years with L.A., winning 17. His lifetime ERA is 3.19. The solid season by this staff was deeply mitigated by the stunning loss to the Giants, as demoralizing to fans as the Bobby Thompson home run in 1951.

# 1963

The retribution, stewed in off-season gloom, came incrementally in baseball style through the long season, but with Koufax and Drysdale leading the charge, it seemed in retrospect in short order and according to the Dodger script. The Dodgers won 99 games in 1963 and swept the Yankees in four straight games in the World Series. (While I missed the televised series because of a thirteen-month vacation in Seoul, South Korea, courtesy of the Eighth Army, I remember listening on the radio at 3:30 a.m. when Koufax won Game 1, 5–2.)

Koufax entered the groove of his first of four straight great years, responsible for his eventual Hall of Fame status. He went 25-5 and won the Triple Crown leading the National League in wins, ERA with 1.88 and strikeouts with 306—in 311 innings. How much better can it get for a pitcher to out-throw everyone in the game and have his team win the pennant and sweep—*sweep!*—the New York Yankees, of all teams, in the World Series? This was the Yankees of Mickey Mantle and Whitey Ford, Roger Maris and Yogi Berra, Elston Howard and Bobby Richardson. "I can see how he won 25 games," Berra said. "What I don't understand is how he lost five." Sportswriter Jim Murray once described the Koufax fastball: "Some batters would start to swing as he was on his way to the mound." Drysdale won 19 games, Podres 14 and Bob Miller 10. Perranoski had his best year, going an incredible 16-3 out of the bullpen, with an ERA of 1.67 with 21 saves. Pete Richert won 5 games, Dick Calmus 3, Roebuck and Nick Wilhite 2 each and Ken Rowe 1.

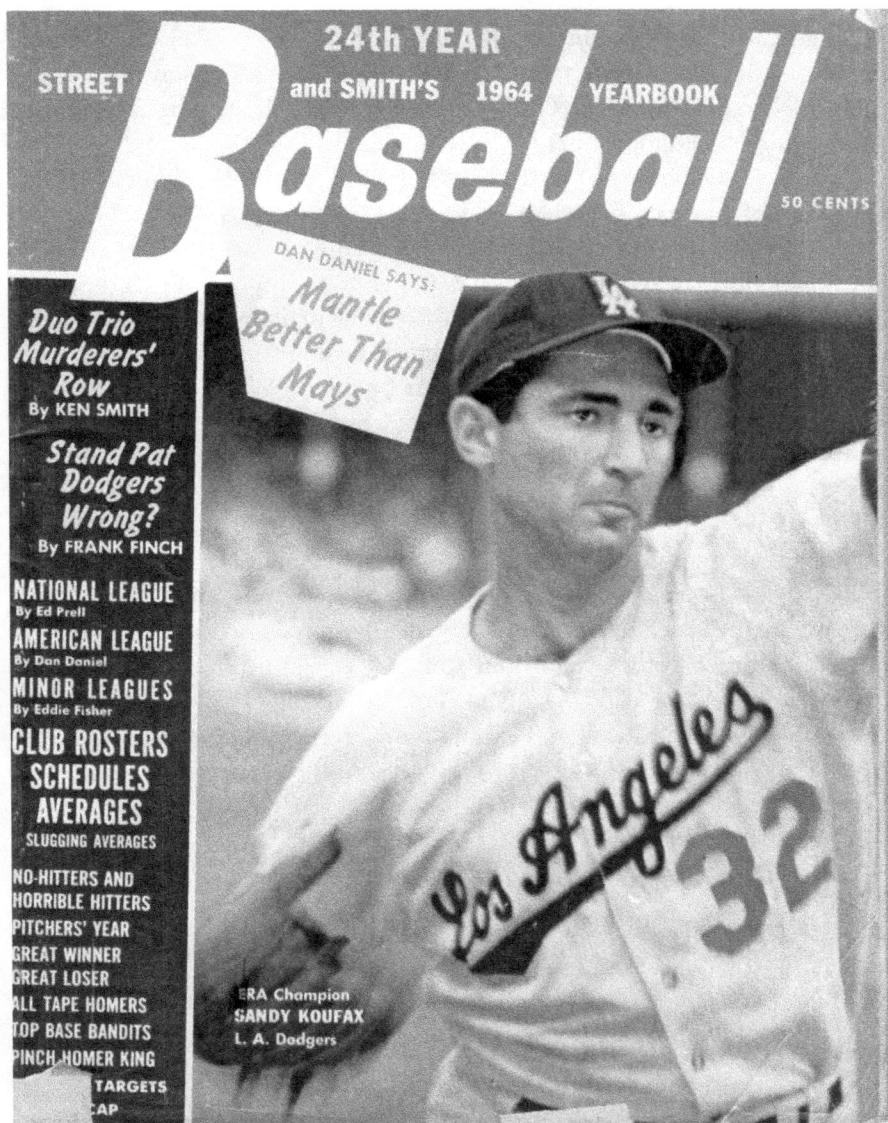

24th YEAR and SMITH'S 1964 YEARBOOK

STREET

**Baseball**

50 CENTS

DAN DANIEL SAYS:

*Mantle Better Than Mays*

**Duo Trio Murderers' Row**
By KEN SMITH

**Stand Pat Dodgers Wrong?**
By FRANK FINCH

**NATIONAL LEAGUE**
By Ed Prell

**AMERICAN LEAGUE**
By Dan Daniel

**MINOR LEAGUES**
By Eddie Fisher

**CLUB ROSTERS SCHEDULES AVERAGES**
SLUGGING AVERAGES

NO-HITTERS AND HORRIBLE HITTERS
PITCHERS' YEAR
GREAT WINNER
GREAT LOSER
ALL TAPE HOMERS
TOP BASE BANDITS
PINCH-HOMER KING
TARGETS
CAP

ERA Champion
SANDY KOUFAX
L. A. Dodgers

On April 18, 1964, Sandy Koufax became only the second pitcher in major-league history to strike out the side with nine pitches in one inning twice. The one pre-Koufax hurler to accomplish the feat was Lefty Grove. Nolan Ryan became the third pitcher to fan three with nine throws in an inning. *Courtesy of the Sporting News Archives.*

Los Angeles native Calmus pitched for the Dodgers in 1963 when he was nineteen years old and went 3-1, and he made one other stay the bigs, a brief 1967 sojourn with the Cubs, without a decision. Wilhite, from Tulsa, Oklahoma, pitched four years for the Dodgers, winning 6 games, 2 in 1963. A Ferndale, Michigan native, Rowe pitched a total of 26 innings in the majors, 14 of those in '63, when he went 1-1.

Of the Dodgers' many incredible moments in 1963, most involved Sandy Koufax. He reduced his walks per nine innings to 1.7, fifth in the league, which was pretty incredible for a power pitcher. On May 11, he had a perfect game going into the eighth inning against archrival San Francisco in spite of the powerful Giants lineup of Willie Mays, Orlando Cepeda, Willie McCovey and Felipe Alou. Sandy walked Ed Bailey on a 3-2 count in the eighth but closed out the Giants in the ninth to preserve his no-hitter.

The 1963 World Series was one that the Yankees would like to permanently forget. Sandy led off the fun with fifteen strikeouts in Game 1. Bobby Richardson struck out three times, and Mickey Mantle, Tom Tresh and Tony Kubek each fanned twice. Reliable Johnny Podres pitched a seven-hitter in Game 2, getting help from Ron Perranoski in the ninth inning to preserve a 4–1 victory. The big guy in Game 3 was Big D—Drysdale pitched a three-hit shutout and won 1–0. Koufax came back in the Game 4 and won 2–1. It capped the most perfect postseason that the Dodgers or nearly any other team could have enjoyed.

# 1964

Another post–World Series malaise came in 1964 as the team only won 80 games. The missing link for half of season was Koufax. On April 18, he became the only pitcher in National League history to have two three-strikeout/nine-pitch innings. On April 22, he felt something "go" in his left arm and needed three cortisone shots. Koufax was 5-4 in early June. On June 4, pitching against the Phillies in Philadelphia, he threw his third no-hitter, winning 3-0. Incredibly, from June to early August, he went 14-1. Then he jammed his arm in August by diving back to second base to beat a pick-off throw. He managed to pitch and win two more games. But the morning after his 19th win, a shutout in which he struck out thirteen, he could not straighten his arm. He was diagnosed by Dr. Robert Kerlan with traumatic arthritis. Sandy was done for the year.

The team's batting average was an anemic .250. Without Koufax, the Dodgers quickly disappeared. Koufax finished at 19-5 with an ERA of 1.74, while Drysdale won 18 with an ERA of 2.19. Lucky they won any with their hitting. Miller, Phil Ortega and Moeller won 7 games apiece. Ortega, who is from Arizona, spent five years with the Dodgers, but the only time he won a game was in 1964. Howie Reed of Dallas, Texas, won 3 games in 1964 and 7 in 1965. He pitched for four other teams, winning another 16 games. He died in 1984 in Texas at age forty-seven. John Purdin, of Lynx, Ohio, played four years for the Dodgers, winning 2 games each in 1964, 1965 and 1968. He died in 2010. The offense consisted of three guys doing what they could. Maury Wills had 173 hits with 53 stolen bases and a batting average of .323, while Willie Davis collected 180 hits with 42 stolen bases. Frank Howard hit 24 homers.

# 1965

The Dodgers had a feast-and-famine year in 1965. Luckily, the famine came first. They righted Walter Alston's ship and won their franchise's fourth World Series, leading the senior circuit with 97 wins. But on the morning of March 31, after pitching a complete game in spring training, Koufax woke to find his arm black and blue from hemorrhaging. He returned to Los Angeles, and team physician Dr. Kerlan told him that he would be lucky to pitch once a week. But Koufax took Empirin with codeine for the pain and Butazolidin for inflammation and used a Capsolin ointment every night. He started 41 games and pitched 335.6 innings, winning his second straight pitching Triple Crown, winning 26 games, posting a 2.04 ERA and striking out 382.

Drysdale went 23-12 with a 2.78 ERA, and newly acquired starter Claude Osteen won 15 games with a 2.79 ERA. Johnny Podres and Howie Reed each won 7, while Miller and Peranoski won 6 each. Also new to the staff was Jim Brewer, who finished at 3-2 with 9 saves. Wilhite was 2-2 and Purdin was 2-1. Mike Kekich, who lost 1 game but went on to pitch nine years in the majors, winning 39 games, and was notable for making news with the Yankees by swapping wives with fellow Yankee hurler Fritz Peterson before the 1973 season. Kekich later broke up with the victim of his amour. (This private life change-up's effect on pitching seemed stifling. Fritz went 8-15 in 1973, and Kekich went 1-1 before being traded to Cleveland, where he was 1-4.) On the Dodgers, Wills piled up 188 hits in 1965. If you can believe it, the leading home run hitters were Jim Lefevbre and Lou Johnson with 12 each. Nobody else did much, but it was enough.

In the World Series, they faced a team of sluggers. The Minnesota Twins, an expansion team in 1961, had managed to make it to the big dance in four years. In 1965, the Twins really blossomed as Tony Oliva won the American League batting title and led in hits, while shortstop Zoilo Versailles led the AL in doubles, triples and total bases. Harmon Killebrew, who had led the league in homers three years running, had an off year with "only" 25 round-trippers and 75 RBIs. They pushed the Dodgers to the seven-game limit, as Mudcat Grant won 2 games and Jim Kaat 1 for Minnesota. Koufax may have drawn the most attention in the series, winning 2 games—the climactic finale, 4–3, with two days' rest—but other heroes emerged.

Wills and Ron Fairly each cracked 11 hits, and the usually light-hitting Wes Parker added 7. When it came down to it, the Dodgers characteristically came up with just enough offense to win. The Twins jumped out to a two-game lead, but both Drysdale and Osteen hurled five-hitters to even the series, and Sandy commanded a four-hitter to put Los Angeles up three games to two. Mudcat Grant hit a home run to help his own cause in a 5–1 Twins victory, setting the stage for Koufax in Game 7.

In the only time that the visiting team won in the series, the Dodgers rode into Minneapolis on the arm of Koufax, who mesmerized the team that led the AL in most offensive categories with a stunning three-hitter. He struck out ten and recorded his second shutout in the series. As seven-game heroics go from the focal point of the mound, it was one of the most dominant performances in history. Koufax was named Most Valuable Player of the series and, later, Sportsman of the Year by *Sports Illustrated*.

# 1966

Somehow the Dodgers won the pennant again in 1966, while Koufax had probably his greatest season: 27-9 with a 1.73 ERA and 317 strikeouts. The only reason he lost 9 games was because of the anemic offense. And then he quit (much more on that later). Claude Osteen won 17 games and Don Sutton 12. But Phil Regan had his greatest year, going 14-1 with an ERA of 1.62. Regan only played three years for the Dodgers and had 27 saves, but that one year made him immortal in Dodger fans' eyes. Perranoski won 6 games, Bob Miller 4 and Moeller 2, and Brewer lost 2 with 2 saves, only pitching twenty-two innings. Offensively, the mighty bat of Jim Lefevbre led the Dodgers with 24 home runs. The World Series, however, was a disaster as the Baltimore Orioles blew the blue away in four straight games.

While this book is a lesson in how far pitching can carry a team, the 1966 World Series was a lesson that pitching can only carry you so far. The American League got revenge for 1963 and L.A.'s destruction of the great Yankees. The Orioles, led by Triple Crown winner Frank Robinson and a team of defensive specialists—Brooks Robinson, Mark Belanger and Paul Blair—allowed only 4 Dodger runs and 17 hits. When a team can only average about 6 hits and 1 run per game, what can you do? Drysdale suffered two of the losses, and Koufax and Osteen dropped one apiece. The Orioles decisively won the first two games in L.A., 5–2 and 6–0, and then gave the Dodgers some of their own medicine: they eked out wins 3 and 4 by 1–0 scores.

# 1967

The next season was the start of some dismal Dodger years without Sandy. Osteen won 17 games, Drysdale 13, Singer 12 and Don Sutton 11. The hitting that didn't arrive for the previous year's World Series was still stranded somewhere. Perranoski won 6, Regan 5 and Miller 2, and Dick Egan, from Berkeley, California, won his only game in four seasons in the Major Leagues. Al Ferrara, "The Bull," led the pathetic offense with a .277 average and 16 homers.

# 1968

The Dodgers improved to 76 wins in 1968 with a great team ERA of 2.69. Drysdale won 14, Singer 13, Osteen 12 and Sutton 11. Drysdale's ERA was 2.15, Sutton's was 2.60 and Singer's was 2.88. Jim Brewer won 8 games and saved 14. Also winning were Regan, Purdin and Kekich with 2 apiece and Foster, Moeller and Hank Aguirre with 1 each. Jack Billingham of Orlando, Florida, won 3 games with an ERA of 2.18 and was let go after that season. He ended up winning 145 games with ten years of double-digit wins, notably with the Cincinnati Reds. Aguirre, born in Azusa in suburban L.A., won 1 game and lost 2 for the Dodgers. He won 75 games in his career, mostly with Detroit, and died in 1994. How the team managed to win any games at all without any offensive support was anyone's guess.

One of the remarkable things of the decade was that the 1968 Dodgers managed to win only 76 games in spite of a pitching staff with a group ERA of 2.69—the second highest in L.A. Dodger history. The incredible

Hall of Famer "Little D" (as opposed to "Big D," Don Drysdale) Don Sutton, won the most games of any L.A. Dodger at 233. He had double-digit wins in twenty-one seasons in the Major Leagues, finishing with 3.09 ERA with the Dodgers and 3.26 ERA lifetime. *Courtesy of the Los Angeles Dodgers.*

staff was led by Drysdale (2.25), Sutton (2.60), Singer (2.88), Osteen (3.08), Brewer (2.49), Mudcat Grant (2.08, brought over from the Twins), Jack Billingham (2.14) and Alan Foster (1.72). Maybe when you hear that the team batting average was .230, some understanding is brought to bear on the issue.

# 1969

In 1969, the Dodgers exploded for 85 wins, led by the pitching of course. Claude Osteen won 20 games with an ERA of 2.66. Bill Singer won 20 with an ERA of 2.34. Don Sutton won 17 games. The only notable thing was that Hall of Fame pitcher Jim Bunning, who recorded excellent seasons with the Detroit Tigers and Philadelphia Phillies but had bombed out in Pittsburgh, won 3 games for L.A. at age 37. The Dodgers threw him back on the market, and he won 10 games back in Philadelphia the next year.

The great Drysdale finished his career at age thirty-two, only two years older than Koufax when he quit. Big D recorded five wins. The Dodgers' decision-making was such that they added castoffs from the Pirates, one of the more notoriously lousy pitching franchises: Bunning was joined by Pete Mikkelson and Al McBean. Mikkelson won 7, Alan Foster 3, McBean 2 and Moeller 1. McBean, who hailed from the Virgin Islands, won 67 games in the majors, pitched 48.1 innings for the Dodgers in 1969 and one inning in 1970.

The most significant thing that happened in 1969 was the retirement of Drysdale. He had torn his rotator cuff at the start of spring training. The defining moment came against Pittsburgh, whose mercurial, line drive–cracking right-fielder Roberto Clemente was notorious for propelling fastballs directly back at the men who threw them, perhaps not in spite. Clemente broke Bob Gibson's leg in 1967 with a line drive. "Roberto Clemente hit a line drive back through the box that could have killed me," Drysdale said in his autobiography. Big D said he brushed the side of his neck and saw his hand "dripping with blood." Clemente's line drive had taken the skin off the edge of his ear. "How's that," he wrote, "for a gentle reminder that you've about had it?"

Clemente only punctuated Drysdale's thoughts with an exclamation point. "I didn't need any X-rays of my shoulder in the summer of '69 to

**STREET and SMITH'S OFFICIAL Yearbook**

*1970* **Baseball** ccc 75¢

**MOST COMPLETE · MOST INFORMATIVE**

CLUB ROSTERS
SCHEDULES
AVERAGES

NATIONAL LEAGUE
By DICK DOZER

AMERICAN LEAGUE
By JOE TRIMBLE

MINOR LEAGUES
By EDDIE FISHER

.300 HITTERS
ARE STILL
DOOMED
By GIL HODGES
Manager, New York Mets

THE GRAND
SLAMMERS
By BOB ADDIE

WEST COAST
THUNDER
By DON MERRY

TOUGHEST TO
STRIKE OUT
By KEN SMITH

THE GREAT
RULES HOAX
By JOE FALLS

SIX FOR SIX
MVP's · GO-GO BOYS
PLAYER'S TARGETS
TOP FIREMEN
SERIES RECAP

BILL SINGER
Los Angeles Dodgers

Bill Singer, who won 20 games in 1969, pitched a no-hitter in 1970 and won 69 games for the Dodgers with a great ERA of 3.03. Bill averaged 7 strikeouts per game and only 2.8 walks. *Courtesy of the Sporting News Archives.*

convince me I had enough," he said. "My teammates must have sensed it too because they gave me a going-away present in San Diego. My last victory was over the Padres on July 28 by a score of 19–0." Imagine that. They gave him enough runs to practically win 20 Dodger games.

When Drysdale decided he could pitch no more, a press conference was held in the Stadium Club, located over the right-field corner of Dodger Stadium, on Monday, August 11, 1969. "Yesterday, when I went upstairs to meet Walter O'Malley," Drysdale said at the press conference, "I sat in the stands to watch a few innings of the game and I heard a sound that I had not heard since I was a boy. In all the years that I pitched, it was as if I'd become immune to the sound of bat hitting ball and ball hitting mitt. It had always been a magnetic click for me and I saw my whole childhood again. I knew then that all my dreams had come true."

He also fulfilled many of the dreams of Dodger faithful. Don Drysdale will be missed forever. Except by the batters who faced him.

# The 1970s

T he Dodgers' superior pitching again mostly prevailed in the 1970s, but there also was reason to rejoice in the decade with the best team-hitting since the Brooklyn era. The Dodgers deployed position players who could also hit, namely the infield of Steve Yeager behind the plate, Steve Garvey at first, Davey Lopes at second, Bill Russell at shortstop and Ron Cey at third. The Dodgers won 910 games in the 1970s, the second-best decade in their history. They won pennants in 1974, 1977 and 1978—three trips to the World Series that they lost, to Oakland once and then twice to the Yankees. Peter O'Malley became president in 1970, and no Dodger team in that decade finished lower than third.

The club's pitching led the majors with a 3.19 ERA across the decade, and L.A. boasted five 20-game winners: Al Downing at 20-9 in 1971; Claude Osteen at 20-11 in 1972; Andy Messersmith at 20-6 in 1974; Don Sutton at 21-10 in 1976; and Tommy John at 20-7 in 1977. Mike Marshall had an incredible year in 1974, setting a major-league record by appearing in 106 games with a 15-12 record and 2.42 ERA, becoming the first relief pitcher in baseball history to win the Cy Young Award. Sutton was on a roll early in the decade, winning 15 in 1970, 17 in 1971, 19 in 1972, 18 in 1973 and 19 in 1974. Adding to the mound mastery were Burt Hooton, winning 18 in 1975 and 19 in 1978, and Andy Messersmith, who won 19 in 1975.

With both leagues split into East and West Divisions for the 1969 season, the Dodgers contended in the West in a mostly decade-long duel with

Cincinnati's formidable "Big Red Machine" for the pennant; the division also included the San Francisco Giants, Atlanta Braves, Houston Astros and San Diego Padres. While the Dodgers regained their poise as one of baseball's best teams in the decade and continued their franchise's great success at the turnstiles as a nonpareil draw, they lost the three World Series to Oakland in 1974 and to the Yankees in the back-to-back years. Steve Garvey won the NL Most Valuable Player Award in 1974 by hitting .312 with 21 homers, 111 RBIs and 200 hits.

The 1970s were also remembered for the winding down of Walter Alston's career as manager—his last year was 1976—and the beginning of Tommy Lasorda's tenure in 1977. Alston, who was voted into the Hall of Fame in 1983 (and passed away the following year), managed the Dodgers for 23 years, winning 2,040 games in the regular season and 23 in the postseason. He also guided the Dodgers to World Series championships in 1955, 1959, 1963 and 1965—three of them in Los Angeles.

Alston inherited a club of Hall of Famers in the 1950s, but he was instrumental in building the 1960s team in Los Angeles, not necessarily from scratch, to win those championships. His great fortune was to have Koufax and Drysdale. But in the 1970s, he literally built the team anew once more, relying some on Osteen and Sutton but bringing the club up from also-rans in the NL West to establish a contender with youthful talent.

Even though the Dodgers were mediocre from 1967 into the 1970s, fans never gave up hope. The owner was Peter O'Malley, the great Walt Alston was manager and players had their moments: with Willie Davis and Wes Parker excelling, help came from Teddy Sizemore; Maury Wills, who strayed to Pittsburgh and the expansion Montreal Expos but was back in blue in 1969; the superb sub Manny Mota; jacks-of-all-trades Jimmy Lefebvre and Bill Sudakis; and youngsters Steve Garvey, Bill Russell and Billy Buckner—all of whom were starting to come into their own.

The mound staff always had go-to intensity, particularly the integral likes of Osteen, Sutton, Singer, Brewer, Moeller and Charley Hough. Nobody seemed to be a prima donna. Osteen and Sutton had played side by side with Koufax and Drysdale, two guys who never transcended team spirit by acting like stars—even though they asked for the big money and knew that they were worth it (and got it). That rubbed off. "Comparing me to Sandy Koufax is like comparing Earl Schieb to Michelangelo," Sutton once said.

Walter (Smokey) Alston managed the Dodgers from 1954 to 1976. He led the Brooklyn Dodgers to victory in the 1955 World Series and then the Los Angeles Dodgers to World Championships in 1959, 1963 and 1965. After he retired, his 2,040 regular-season managerial wins were topped only by Connie Mack, John J. McGraw, Casey Stengel and Bucky Harris. *Courtesy of the Los Angeles Dodgers.*

# 1970

The Dodgers won 87 games in 1970, coming in second in the West, 14½ games behind the Reds. Reliable Claude Osteen won 16 games with an ERA of 3.83. Sutton came back with 15 wins, and Alan Foster proved his worth and won 10. Foster, who was born near Pasadena, made his fourth year with the Dodgers his best. He moved on after that year to win 34 more games with four teams in six years. Moeller won 7 games and Singer 8. Pete Mikkelson went 4-2. Freddie Norman won 2 games and was let go. He went on to win 106 games in the next fifteen years for four other teams.

Also winning games for the Dodgers were Sandy Vance with 7, Ray Lamb with 6, Jose Pena with 4 and Mike Strahler with 1. Vance, who was born in Lamar, Colorado, won 9 games in two years and was out of baseball. Lamb, from Glendale, California, pitched three more years and was gone. Pena, who hailed from Mexico, pitched three years for the blue, winning a total of 6 games. Chicagoan Strahler was on the L.A. staff for three years and won 2 games. The great fielding first baseman Wes Parker surprised the faithful by hitting .319, and Willie Davis had 181 hits. Nobody else did much.

# 1971

The 1971 season remains a mystery because the Dodgers won 89 games, but some of the faithful still don't know how it was done. The most remarkable thing was that Gentleman Al Downing, who had won 2 games the previous year, came to the Dodgers and won 20 big ones with an ERA of 2.68. The guy was superb. The most games he had won previously was 14 with the Yankees, and he never won more than 9 in a season thereafter. Sutton won 17, Osteen 11, Singer 10 and Mikkelson 8.

Reliable Jim Brewer logged 22 saves and an ERA of 1.88. Hoyt Wilhelm, a relief legend, pitched his final two years with the Dodgers at ages forty-eight and forty-nine. In 1971, he entered in games twice and had an ERA of 1.02. He pitched for 22 years with one of the lowest ERAs in baseball history, 2.52. Doyle Alexander started with the Dodgers in 1971 and won 6 games. He then went to Baltimore and on to a career with nine different teams in 18 years. He won 194 games and has a lifetime ERA of 3.76 with

Al Downing is known as the pitcher who tossed up the baseball that Hank Aaron clouted in 1974 for the all-time home run record of 715, passing Babe Ruth. But Downing also won 46 games for L.A., including 20 in 1971. *Courtesy of the Los Angeles Dodgers.*

seasons of double-figures in wins, twice with 17. Pena, Vance, the enduring Moeller and Bob O'Brien each won 2. O'Brien, who came from Pittsburgh's system, lasted one year in the bigs.

The Dodgers were kind of offensive for a change, with Willie Davis getting 198 hits and Dick Allen, formerly "Richie" Allen with the Phillies, hitting 23 homers. The year also marked the arrival of one of the most promising talent pools in Dodger history: Bobby Valentine, Bill Buckner, Steve Garvey, Bill Russell, Billy Grabarkewitz, Bill Sudakis, Von Joshua, Willie Crawford and Tom Paciorek. The oldest guy in that group was Grabby at twenty-five. Buckner made the biggest splash, getting 99 hits with a .277 average.

# 1972

In 1972, that core group was augmented by Davey Lopes and Ron Cey. The team won 85 games, led by Osteen's 20-win season and supplemented by Sutton's 19 and Tommy John's 11. John, who had led the American League twice in shutouts, was acquired from the White Sox. Downing posted 9 wins, Brewer 8 and 17 saves, Singer 6 wins, Mikkelson 5, Perranoski and Richert 2 apiece and Strahler 1. The reliable Doug Rau arrived on the scene to notch 2 victories. Willie Davis had 178 hits and 19 homers. Hall of Famer Frank Robinson, who had been the Orioles' big gun in 1966, the year they swept the Dodgers in the World Series, hit 19 home runs. But the Dodgers let him go, and he went on to hit 64 more home runs in five years before quitting.

# 1973

In 1973, the Dodger infield of the future started to play regularly together—Garvey, Lopes, Russell and Cey—and lasted as a group through 1981. The Dodgers won 95 games in 1973, which still wasn't enough to unseat the Reds as division champion. L.A. came in second again, 3½ games behind Cincinnati. Sutton was on the hill for 18 victories, and John and Osteen for 16 apiece, while the newly acquired

Andy Messersmith won 14. Downing won 9 and Brewer 6, with 20 saves. Hough won 4, Richert 3 and Geoff Zahn 1. Zahn went on to win 111 games in thirteen seasons, with his best in 1982 when he logged 18 wins for the California Angels. He only played one more year for the Dodgers, winning 3 games. The hitting load was shared by Lopes, Russell, Cey, Davis and Joe Ferguson.

# 1974

In 1974, the Dodgers won their first pennant since 1966 by putting up 102 victories, their most since 1962, and 4 games in front of the Reds. The team's ERA, 2.97, was the best in the National League. The pitching staff finished first in the league with the fewest number of hits (1,272), runs (561) and bases on balls (464) given up, as well as the most strikeouts (943). Messersmith won 20 games and Sutton 19.

Mike Marshall came aboard from Montreal to win 15 games and save 24 in an unbelievable 106 appearances, 13 of them consecutively in relief. The total appearances and consecutive appearances still stand as major-league records. He had knocked around the American League before becoming an Expo in 1970 and honing his relief skills. The Dodgers' foresight in acquiring him and using him as an immediate, integral part of their pitching protected the aces and turned around many games. The team might not have approached 85 or 90 wins without him and certainly wouldn't have broken the century mark. His Cy Young Award that year was certainly earned. Tommy John and Doug Rau both won 13 games, Hough 9, Downing 5, Brewer 4, Zahn 3 and Rick Rhoden 1. The team led the NL in runs scored (798) and home runs (a paltry 139). Garvey hit .312 with 200, 111 RBIs and 21 homers. The "Toy Cannon," muscular Jimmy Wynn, acquired from the Houston Astros, hit 32 homers and was named NL Comeback Player of the Year. Buckner, Lopes, Cey, Russell, Willie Crawford and Joe Ferguson all had creditable years.

Sutton had a 9-game winning streak during the year and won both the opener and the clincher in the best-of-five National League Playoff Series against the champion Pirates of the East. The Bucs were known as the "Lumber Company" and paced the Major Leagues in team hitting at .274, led by Willie Stargell, Al Oliver and Rennie Stennett. But the Dodgers sawed up the lumber in four games, with Messersmith winning Game 2.

**STREET and SMITH'S OFFICIAL Yearbook**

*1975* **Baseball**

ccc
02050
$1.00

**MOST COMPLETE · MOST INFORMATIVE**

CLUB ROSTERS
SCHEDULES
AVERAGES

MIKE MARSHALL
Los Angeles Dodgers

AMERICAN LEAGUE
By DICK DOZER

NATIONAL LEAGUE
By ROSS NEWHAN

MINOR LEAGUES
By BOB SNYDER

*LOU BROCK
SPURS YEAR
OF BIG STEAL*
By BOB ADDIE

*BASEBALL'S
FASTEST
PITCHERS*
By DON MERRY

*SUICIDE
SQUEEZE*
By KEN SMITH

*HITTING FOR
THE CYCLE*
By CHARLEY FEENEY

FRANK ROBINSON
DESIGNATED HITTERS
MVP'S
INCIDENTALLY
LONGEST GAMES
TOP FIREMEN
PLAYERS' TARGETS
SERIES RECAP

Mike Marshall set the record for most appearances by a relief pitcher in one year—106 in 1974. He won 15 games and saved 21. He also holds the major-league record for relief in the most consecutive games, 13. *Courtesy of the Sporting News Archives.*

The blue, however, lost the World Series in five games to flamboyant owner Charlie Finley's Oakland A's, who were publicly squabbling with him and one another. It was a volatile bunch, with Reggie Jackson, Vida Blue, Rollie Fingers and Catfish Hunter, but they didn't fight enough to derail their dynasty's third and final World Series victory in a row. It was a strange series. Four of the games were decided by 3–2 scores and Game 4 by a 5–2 result. Ken Holtzman pitched the first game for the A's against Messersmith, and Fingers won the game in relief at Dodger Stadium. Sutton prevailed against Vida Blue with a shutout until the ninth, when he allowed two runs. Marshall stepped up for the save. In the third game, in Oakland Coliseum, Catfish Hunter beat Al Downing. Holtzman returned to the mound in the fourth game to give Messersmith his second loss of the series. Sutton started against Blue Moon Odom in the fifth game, which was lost by Marshall.

# 1975

While L.A. didn't win in the pinnacle series, the team firmly reestablished itself as one of baseball's most potent franchises, a contender with a brand of top-notch pitching that had brought it to the big dance in past campaigns. However, the year 1975 brought a drop in victories to 88, as they finished second, 20 games behind the runaway Big Red Machine. But the pitching, of course, was tough. The team finished number one in ERA, complete games (51) and the fewest number of hits (1,215), runs (534) and bases on balls (448) allowed.

Messersmith won 19 games, Burt Hooton 18, Sutton 16 and Rau 15. Marshall won 9 games out of the bullpen, Jim Brewer, Rick Rhoden and Charlie Hough won 3 apiece and Al Downing won 2. A former bitter archenemy was brought onto the Dodger staff to pitch three innings and lose a game: Juan Marichal, the same San Francisco Giant great who hit John Roseboro over the head with a bat in 1965. This Hall of Famer won 243 games in 16 seasons, and his brief tryst with the Dodgers was his swan song. Garvey showed up big again with 210 hits, 18 homers and 95 RBIs. Lopes and Cey also had decent years.

**Street & Smith's Official 1979 Yearbook**

39th YEAR    $1.95

**Baseball**

*Most Complete*    *Most Informative*

CLUB ROSTERS
SCHEDULES
AVERAGES

AMERICAN LEAGUE
By Dick Dozer
NATIONAL LEAGUE
By Phil Collier
MINOR LEAGUES
By Bob Snyder

ROSE'S RUN
FOR JOE D's
STREAK
By Bob Addie

RIFLE-ARMED
OUTFIELDERS
By Ken Smith

SPEEDIEST
CATCHERS AND
OTHER BASE
BANDITS

TAPE HOMERS

WHIFFS BY BATTERS
WHIFFS BY PITCHERS

NO HITTERS AND
DOUBLE NO HITTER

ROOKIE RECORDS
CLUB BATTING

PLAYER'S TARGETS
MVP'S
TOP FIREMEN
SERIES RECAP

BURT HOOTON
Los Angeles Dodgers

Coming off his 1978 season, Burt Hooton was considered one of baseball's best pitchers. He was 19-10 that year with a 2.71 ERA. He was second in winning percentage (.665) to San Diego's Gaylord Perry (.778). *Courtesy of the Sporting News Archives.*

# 1976

The Dodgers won 92 games in 1976 but finished behind the Reds again, 10 games off the pennant mark. Sutton had one of his best years, winning 21 games. Rau won 16, Rhoden and Hough 12 apiece, Hooton 11 and Tommy John 10. Mike Marshall won 4 in relief and Al Downing 1. But three staffers were added: Stan Wall and Elias Sosa, who won 2 games each, and Dennis Lewallyn, who won 1. Wall, who hailed from Missouri, pitched three years in the bigs, winning 2 again in 1977 and 1978. Sosa won 59 games in the majors in twelve seasons but only spent 1976 and 1977 with the Dodgers, during which time he won 2 games each year. Lewallyn is either an unusual or typical case, depending on how you view the vicissitudes of the pitching game. The guy spent eight years in the majors, pitching a total of eighty innings and finishing 4-4. Garvey brought stability to the offense, with 200 hits again and a .317 average. A superb hitter with power, he undoubtedly would have posted 100 RBIs every year if he had played for the Reds or Pirates. Buckner had 193 hits and a .301 average.

Knuckleballer Charlie Hough pitched eleven years for the Dodgers and won 47 games while posting a 3.42 ERA. His best year for L.A. was 1976, when he went 12-8. He won 216 games and lost 216 in his twenty-five-year career. *Courtesy of the Los Angeles Dodgers.*

# 1977

After Tommy Lasorda became manager for the 1977 season, there was no doubt that he was a big blowhard. But he managed to capture the allegiance of the fans as well as the team. He might be Lasorda, and all the blabbity-blab that being Lasorda represents, but he certainly was L.A.'s Lasorda. "You could plant two thousand rows of corn with the fertilizer he spreads around," said television baseball announcer and former catcher Joe Garagiola. There was no doubt that he did indeed bleed Dodger blue. As a former Dodger pitcher, he went way back, to the Brooklyn clubs of 1954 and 1955, when he pitched in four games each year with no decisions. He eventually posted a 0-4 career record after a year with the Kansas City A's (before they moved to Oakland).

The stout holler guy quickly proved himself vastly more superior in the managerial ranks than on the mound. He inherited a load of talent and followed the tenet that if it's not broke, don't fix it. Lasorda led L.A. back to the top in 1977 as the pitching staff again reigned with the top ERA in league (3.22). The pitchers also led the NL in fewest runs (582) and fewest bases on balls (438) allowed. Tommy John had a banner year with 20 wins. Rhoden won 16, and Sutton and Rau won 14 each, while Hooton posted 12 victories and Hough 6. Lance Rautzhan and Mike Garman won 4 apiece, Lewallyn 3, Sosa and Wall 2 each and Bobby Castillo 1. Rautzhan, who hails from Pottsville, Pennsylvania, spent three seasons in the majors, winning 6 games for the Dodgers. Garman, of Caldwell, Idaho, has a lifetime mark of 22-27 and somehow lasted nine years in the majors—shades of Lewallyn. The big news offensively was that four Dodgers hit 30 or more home runs: Garvey with 33, Reggie Smith with 32 and Ron Cey and Dusty Baker with 30 each. Garvey had 115 RBIs and Cey 110.

L.A. won the best-of-five NL Championship Series over Philadelphia after the Phillies took the opener, 7–5. Sutton, Rautzhan and Tommy John picked up the wins in the first of two successive years in which L.A. derailed the Phillies of the Mike Schmidt era 3 games to 1 for the honor of losing the World Series to the dingbat Yankees of the Reggie Jackson era, 4 games to 2. It wasn't quite like tape-recording 1977 and replaying it in 1978, but it was close.

Jackson batted .450 in the series, and most of his 9 hits (5) went over the fence, 3 in the sixth and final contest at Yankee Stadium. This is where the legend of "Mr. October" comes from. Sutton started against Don Gullett

Tommy Lasorda, who was said to "bleed Dodger blue," led L.A. to pennants in his first full season in 1977 and again in 1978. His teams won the World Series in 1981 and 1988. *Courtesy of the Los Angeles Dodgers.*

and lost the first game, 4–3. Burt Hooton bested former A's ace Catfish Hunter, 6–1, in the second game. Mike Torrez beat Tommy John at Dodger Stadium, 5–3. In Game 4, Ron Guidry outdueled Doug Rau, 4–2. The Dodgers came back in Game 5 behind Don Sutton to rip the Yankees, 10–4. But Torrez hurled the capper and beat Hooton in Game 6, 8–4, with a little help from Mr. October.

# 1978

Lasorda led the team to its second straight National League pennant in 1978. They dispatched the Phillies again as Steve Garvey chipped in with 4 home runs, and Sutton, John and Terry Forster collected the wins. However, they lost to the Yankees again, 4–2, *after* winning the first 2 games. Hooton won 19 games, John 17, Rau and Sutton 15 and Rhoden 10 in the regular season. Bob Welch added 7, Hough and Forster 5 apiece and Rautzhan 2. Once again the Dodgers led in team ERA (3.12), allowing the fewest runs (573).

In the World Series, the Dodgers blasted 15 hits in the first game, including homers by Dusty Baker and Davey Lopes, to win, 11–5, at Dodger Stadium behind Tommy John. Then Burt Hooton beat Catfish Hunter, 4–3, followed by the Yankees winning their first of four straight, 5–1, behind Ron Guidry in Game 3 at Yankee Stadium. Rich Gossage saved Game 4, 4–3, beating reliever Bob Welch. The universally renowned Jim Beattie, who was 6-9 that year, beat Hooton and the Dodgers, 12–2, as the Yanks pounded out 18 hits in Game 5. Back at Dodger Stadium, the Yankees won their fourth game in the row as Catfish Hunter defeated Sutton, 7–2. The mighty Bucky Dent was named the Most Valuable Player, hitting .417 in the series after having tallied .243 in the regular season. Mr. October only cracked 2 homers but got 9 hits again (.391), with 8 RBIs.

# 1979

In 1979, with basically the same team, the Dodgers were mediocre, placing third in the NL West behind Cincinnati and Houston, winning 79 games. Rick Sutcliffe, who was the L.A. Dodgers' first pitcher to be named Rookie of the Year, won 17 games. Since its inception in 1949, fifteen Dodgers have been named Rookie of the Year (twelve in L.A.), by far the most in the majors. (The Yankees, by contrast, have won 8.) Four Dodger pitchers have won the coveted award—including Steve Howe in 1980, Fernando Valenzuela in 1981 and Hideo Nomo in 1995—but Sutcliffe was the first.

Sutton won 12 games in 1979 and Hooton 11. Charlie Hough and Jerry Reuss won 7 apiece, Bob Welch 5, Dave Patterson and Ken Brett 4 each, Bobby Castillo and Andy Messersmith 2 apiece and Joe Beckwith, Terry Forster and Doug Rau 1 each. Patterson, of Springfield, Missouri, spent one year in the majors, going 4-1. Ken Brett, one of the great Brett brothers from El Segundo, California, spent fourteen years in the bigs, won 83 games and lost 85. In his one year with his hometown Dodgers, he went 4-3 with an ERA of 3.45. Not bad. While he registered an identical 13-9 back-to-back in 1973 and 1974 with Philadelphia and Pittsburgh and won 13 games another time, in 1977, when he was shared by the White Sox and Angels, his biggest claim to fame was as a brother to George Brett, the Hall of Famer who won three batting titles in 21 years with the Kansas City Royals. Ken Brett died in 2003 after a six-year battle with brain cancer. He was fifty-five.

Beckwith, of Auburn, Alabama, won 9 games in five years with the Dodgers. He lasted sixteen years in the big leagues, winning 54 games. His ERA was 3.23, which is what kept him in the majors. Forster, from Sioux Falls, South Dakota, lasted sixteen seasons, also winning 54 games. Listen, it seems to be a big deal if you can just last some innings in the majors. If you can pitch effectively every once in a while, you can go on pitching for years. The most games Forster ever won in a season was 7 for the White Sox (in the same year, 1974, that he led the AL in saves with 24). His lifetime ERA was 3.23. He won 11 games for the Dodgers in five years. Garvey sprayed 204 hits, and Lopes had probably his best year, hitting an impressive 28 homers while stealing 44 bases and scoring 109 runs.

# The 1980s

The 1980s formed the Dodgers' last solid decade to date. As in the 1950s and 1960s, they managed to win the World Series twice—in the strike-shortened 1981 season with the timely arrival of Fernando Valenzuela and the hard work of Burt Hooton and Jerry Reuss, as well as in 1988, due to the heroics of the incredible Orel Hershiser. They also won their division in 1985 after a season of 95 wins but lost in the National League Championship Series to the St. Louis Cardinals in the deciding Game 5.

A burly, fireballing lefty, Valenzuela set Los Angeles on its ear and brought out more Hispanic fans to Dodger Stadium than in any other time. "Fernando-mania" not only caught on in L.A. but also brought the spotlight on young Fernando and the Dodgers in a decade in which baseball could use a popularity booster because of disgust generated by the labor strike. The negotiations were characterized by some as a case of millionaires seeking to become multimillionaires, the fans be damned. Valenzuela's immediate fame and his humble beginnings in Sonora, Mexico, made him a fan favorite everywhere. He also was only one of two 20-game winners for Los Angeles in the 1980s, going 21-11 in 1986. Hershiser was 23-8 in 1988.

The Dodgers kept putting Rookie of the Year winners on the field. Their players won the award in three straight years: Valenzuela (1981), Steve Howe (1982) and second sacker Steve Sax (1982). Left-hander Jerry Reuss pitched a no-hitter on June 27, beating San Francisco, 8–0. The worst thing that the 1980s brought was the demise of their great infield. Davey Lopes's last year was 1981, before he moved on to Oakland. Steve Garvey signed with the

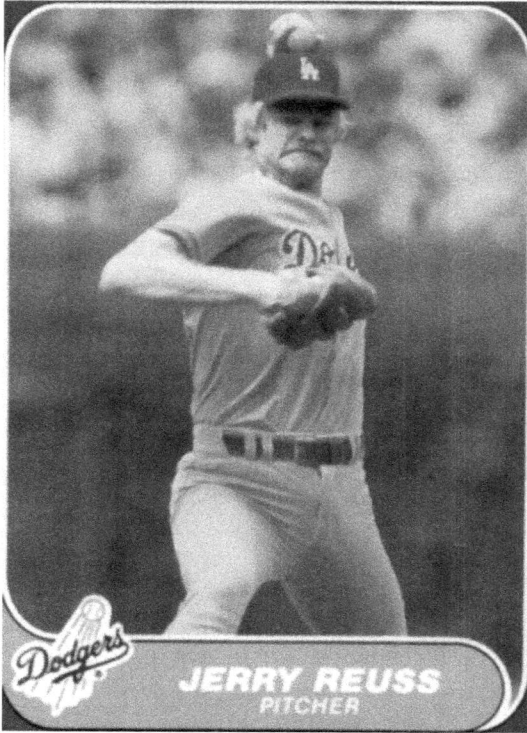

Jerry Reuss was a great Dodger leftie who won 86 games for L.A. with a 2.12 ERA. He also won 18 games in 1980 and 1982 and pitched a no-hitter against the San Francisco Giants in 1980, 8–0. *Courtesy of Upper Deck.*

San Diego Padres in December 1982. Third baseman Ron Cey's last year was 1982 before going to the Chicago Cubs, with whom he enjoyed four more good seasons. Catcher Steve Yeager's last year was 1985. Shortstop Bill Russell lasted through 1986 before retiring. Also, one of the franchise's signature moments occurred in the decade, when Kirk Gibson, injured and supposedly out of action, practically came off his deathbed to hit a home run and drive the Dodgers toward an eventual World Series win.

# 1980

The Dodgers won 92 games in 1980, finishing second to the Houston Astros. The Dodgers placed second in the league in ERA with 3.25 but finished first in fewest hits allowed (1,358) and most shutouts (15). Jerry

Reuss won 18 games, Hooton and Welch won 14 apiece and good old Don Sutton, at age thirty-five, went 13-5 with an ERA of 2.21. Bobby Castillo won 8 games, Dave Golz and Steve Howe 7 each, Joe Beckwith and Rick Sutcliffe 3 apiece, a guy by the name of Fernando Valenzuela along with Don Stanhouse 2 each and Charlie Hough 1. Goltz, who came from Pelican, Minnesota, had won 96 games for Minnesota in eight years, including 20 in 1977. His acquisition was characterized by the Dodgers as the hiring of a savior, but in two years, he won 9 games and lost 18 with an ERA over 4.00 and was paid really big bucks. Stanhouse, out of Du Quoin, Illinois, pitched one year for the Dodgers and finished 2-2. He had 38 wins in ten seasons. Offensively, some spark and power showed as Garvey collected 200 hits with a .304 average, 26 homers and 106 RBIs. Dusty Baker had a good year with 179 hits, 39 homers and 97 RBIs. Ron Cey hit 28 home runs.

# 1981

The year 1981 was crazy and remarkable for the Dodgers. "Fernando-mania" had a lot to do with that. On opening day, rookie pitcher Valenzuela, replacing an injured Jerry Reuss, hurled a 2-0 shutout of Pittsburgh. Toward the end of April, Valenzuela had pitched 4 shutouts in five starts, was 5-0 with a 0.20 ERA and was batting .438. By the end of May, the turnstiles at Dodger Stadium had admitted 1 million fans in twenty-two home dates—the earliest that a major-league stadium had reached that attendance mark in any season. While Fernando tapered off a bit from his superior performance skein, he was the baseball story of the year.

Fernando went on to post one of the best Dodger seasons ever. He won not only Rookie of the Year but also the Cy Young Award as the NL's best pitcher; he was the first rookie to ever win that award. Fernando finished 13-7 in the strike-shortened season with 11 complete games and 8 shutouts. His ERA was 2.48, and he collected 180 strikeouts as the first rookie to lead either league in strikeouts since Herb Score in 1955. Fernando pitched 192.1 innings, and he also hit .250. And he beat the Yankees, 5–4, in Game 3 to turn the tide of the World Series.

Fernando Valenzuela incited "Fernandomania" just by walking out to the mound in 1981. In his first start, he five-hit the Houston Astros. He recorded 4 shutouts in his first five starts and had 8 for the year for a National League rookie record. *Courtesy of the Sporting News Archives.*

# Seven Decades of Diamond Dominance

The ballplayers went out on strike for seven weeks and one day. The team was second in ERA (3.01), and first in shutouts (15) and complete games (26). Hooten won 11 and Reuss 10. Bob Welch had 9 wins, Howe 5, Dave Stewart 4, Tom Niedenfurer 3, Sutcliff and Castillo 2 apiece and Alejandro Pena and Ted Power 1 each. Dave Stewart was a very irritating guy. He never did much for the Dodgers. He was all promise and no delivery. He pitched 191 innings for L.A. and walked 113 batters. So the Dodgers got rid of him, and he continued on a journeyman's career until he developed the forkball to supplement his fastball and slider. He won 20 or more games four years in a row and ended up with 168 wins in sixteen years. He led the Oakland Athletics to three straight World Series. He had the temerity to develop late.

The Dodgers ended their relationship with Sutcliffe as well. He, by the way, went to Chicago Cubs, where he was 16-1 in 1984, winning the Cy Young Award. Sutcliffe also won 171 games in eighteen seasons, which would have made him third all-time on the L.A. Dodger list—ahead of Koufax. Some guys need changes of scenery. Power (a great baseball name), from Oklahoma, won 2 games for the Dodgers in two years and then went on to win 66 games in 11 more seasons—also not for the Dodgers. Pedro Guerrero hit .300 and Dusty Baker .315 in the strike-shortened season. No one else did much.

The playoffs were a kick. Due to the strike at midseason, the year was broken into halves, and the winner of the first half-season played the winner of the second half in each of the four NL and AL divisions, much to the consternation of the Cincinnati Reds, who had the best overall NL West record for the whole season but came in second in both half-seasons. So, the first-half winner, L.A., played the second half–winning Astros. After losing the first two games of the best-of-five series in Houston (3–1 to Nolan Ryan and 1–0 to Joe Sambito), the Dodgers swept the last three in Dodger Stadium. As usual, the Dodgers had to depend on pitching. But reliable Hooton won Game 3, 6–1, Fernando won Game 4, 2–1, and Reuss pitched a shutout to win the finale, 4–0. Against Montreal in the National League Championship Series (NLCS), Hooten won the first game, beating Bill Gullickson, 5–1. Strange as it may seem, Ray Burris shut out Fernando, 3–0, in Game 2. Montreal also won Game 3 as Steve Rogers beat Reuss. But the Dodgers came back to win Game 4, 7–1, behind Hooten—again. Fernando won the finale, 2–1, thanks to Rick Monday's two-out home run in the ninth inning.

The World Series was the same come-from-behind situation. Again, the Dodgers lost the first two games of the series—to Ron Guidry and their old compadre, Tommy John, who had joined the Yankees for the 1979 season. Fernando righted the team in Game 3, winning 5–4. Steve Howe saved Game 4. Reuss won Game 5, 2–1, and the Dodgers polished off the Yanks, 9–2, behind Hooten, with relief help from Howe at Yankee Stadium. It was the Dodgers' sixth World Championship, counting the one in 1900 in Brooklyn, and their fourth in Los Angeles in just over two decades.

# 1982

The 1982 season was unremarkable. The post–World Series malaise can again be invoked—except that Valenzuela won 19 games with an ERA of 2.87. The Dodgers won 88 games, 18 courtesy of Reuss and 16 from Bob Welch. The team also led the league in ERA again (3.26) and in shutouts (13), innings pitched (1488.1) and fewest home runs allowed (81). Stewart totaled 9 wins, Howe 7, Forster 5, Hooton 4, Niedenfurer 3, Beckwith and Ricky Wright 2 apiece and Power, Steve Shirley and Vincente Romo with 1 each. Wright, from Paris, Texas, pitched two years for the Dodgers and won as many games. Shirley, from San Francisco, pitched one year for the Dodgers. Romo, a Mexico native, pitched eight years in the majors, his last for the Dodgers, winning 1 game. Steve Sax, who became the fourth consecutive Dodger to win Rookie of the Year, collected 180 hits while Pedro Guerrero hit .304, with 32 home runs and 100 RBIs.

# 1983

In 1983, the Dodgers won 91 games, with Fernando and Welch getting 15 wins apiece and Pena and Reuss 12 each. Hooton recorded 9, Niedenfurer 8, Pat Zachry 6, Stewart 5, Howe 4, Beckwith 3 and Rick Honeycutt 2. Zachry, out of Richmond, Texas, won 11 games in two years for the Dodgers and finished his career with 69 wins in ten years. The Dodgers—ho-hum—had the best ERA again (3.10). Guerrero again hit 32 home runs. But for the third time in seven years in the NLCS, they lost to the Phillies, three games to one. Philadelphia ace Steve Carlton outdueled Reuss, 1–0, in the first game.

Fernando won the second, 4–1. Philadelphia put up identical 7–2 scores in the final two games, the last one behind Carlton, to earn the right to get beat by Baltimore in a five-game World Series.

# 1984

The Dodgers faltered in 1984, winning 79 games for an ignominious fourth-place finish in the NL West. But the staff finished first in complete games (39) and first in fewest home runs allowed (76) and most strikeouts (1,033). Bob Welch paced the team with 13 wins, while Alejandro Pena and Valenzuela posted 12 apiece, Hershiser 11 and Honeycutt 10. Ken Howell, Zachry and Reuss had 5 victories apiece, Hooton 3, Niedenfuer 2 and Carlos Diaz 1. Diaz, who was born in Hawaii, won 7 games for the Dodgers in three years. The anemic offense was led by Mike Marshall—the *other* Mike Marshall, the outfielder and occasional first baseman, not the great reliever in a retooled career—with 21 homers.

Carlos Diaz, who was born in Hawaii, pitched three years for the Los Angeles Dodgers, winning 7 games and saving 1. *Courtesy of Upper Deck.*

# 1985

The year 1985 was a great one for the Dodgers as they won 95 games, 5.5 games in front of the waning Big Red Machine, and led the league with an ERA of 2.96. The staff also was first in complete games (37), shutouts (16) and fewest hits allowed (1,280). Orel Hershiser really started warming up in 1985 as he collected 19 wins. "Bull Dog" Hershiser was a great Dodger pitcher, with guts, intelligence and a high likability quotient during interviews. He was a real fan favorite, especially for me. There are not many Dodgers I have liked more. Orel was an incredible 19-3, leading the league with an .864 winning percentage and a wonderful 2.03 ERA. Dwight Gooden went 24-4 for the Mets with an ERA of a minuscule 1.53 and won the Cy Young Award. Welch was a great 13-4 with an ERA of 2.31. Reuss won 14, Honeycutt 8, Niedenfuer 7, Diaz 6, Ken Howell 4, Castillo 2 and Howe, Dennis Powell, Brian Holton and Tom Brennan 1 apiece. Powell, out of Moultrie, Georgia, is another pitcher who lasted eight seasons, winning a total of 11 games, 3 with the Dodgers. Brennan of Chicago, Illinois, spent five years in the majors, finishing his career with the Dodgers, winning 1 and losing 2. Holton, out of McKeesport, Pennsylvania, pitched four years for the Dodgers through 1988, winning 13 games. He pitched two more years for Baltimore and retired.

Guerrero clubbed 33 homers and batted .320, while Mike Marshall hit 28 homers and hit .293. Those were the bright spots, and L.A. still won 95 games, which illustrates what a good pitching can do. The Dodgers faced St. Louis in the National League playoffs, which had expanded to a best-of-seven format. Los Angeles won the first two games handily behind Fernando and Orel, who threw 4–1 and 8–2 victories, respectively. Then they lost four games in a row, with Welch and Reuss getting the losses in the first pair and Niedenfurer responsible for the final two. This four-game skid made the World Series an all-Missouri affair—as the George Brett–led Kansas City Royals beat the Cards in seven games.

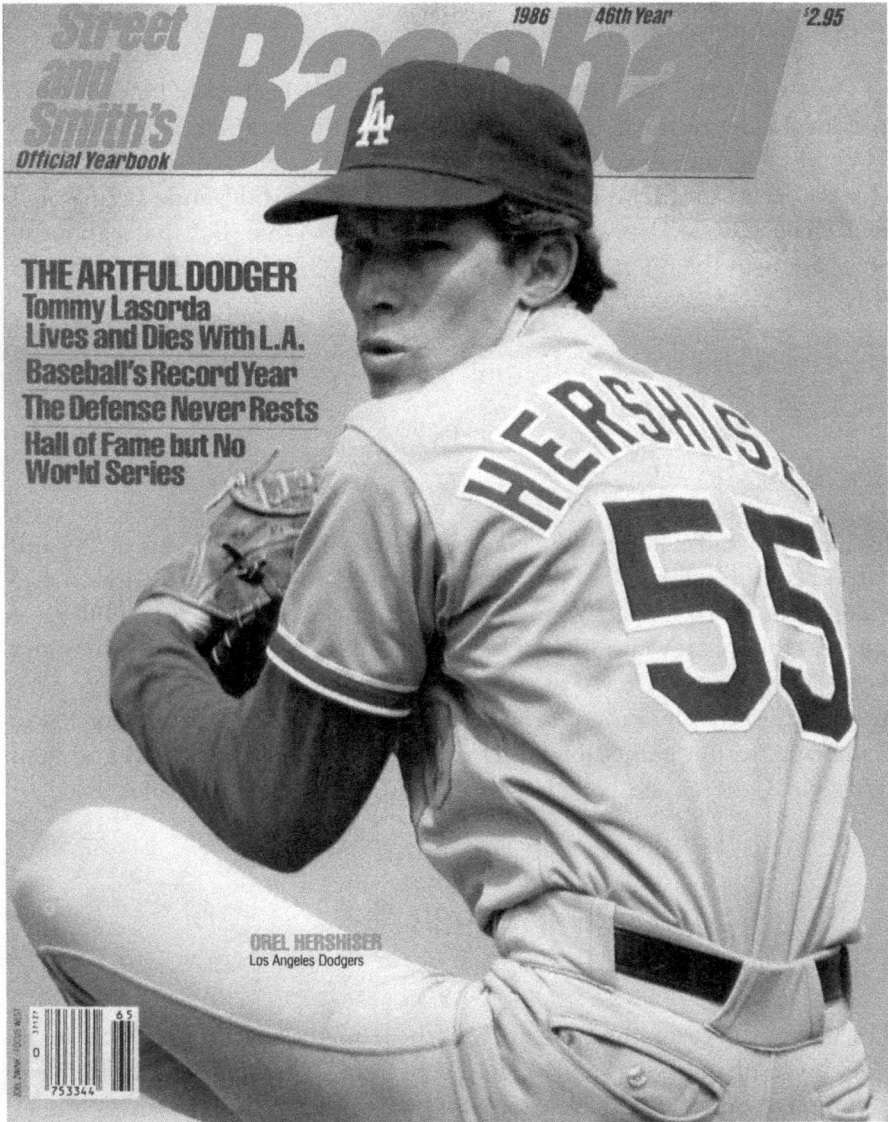

The Dodgers clinched the 1985 NL West title on October 2 when Orel Hershiser hurled a 9–3 win over the Atlanta Braves for his 19th victory. Hershiser went 19-3 that year and led the NL with an .864 winning percentage. *Courtesy of the Sporting News Archives.*

# 1986

In 1986 and 1987, the Dodgers sunk to 73 wins in each year, for fifth place and fourth, respectively, in the six-team NL West. In 1986, Fernando won 21 games, Hershiser 14 and Honeycutt 11. Welch won 7, Niedenfurer 6 and Holton, Reuss and Powell 2 apiece, while Pena and Ed Vande Berg won 1 each. The staff led the league in complete games (35), but that's about it. Steve Sax was the offense, with 210 hits and a .332 average. Everyone else? Forget it.

# 1987

In 1987, the staff again led the National League in complete games (29) and earned runs (601). Hershisher stepped up with 16 wins, Welch with 15 and Valenzuela with 14. Matt Young won 5; Tim Belcher and Shawn Hillegas 4 apiece; Holton, Howell and Tim Leary 3 each; Pena 2; and Niedenfurer and Tim Crews 1 each. Crews, of Tampa, Florida, won 11 games in six years. Young was 5-8 in his only year with the Dodgers. Hillegas, from Dos Palos, California, won 4 games for the Dodgers in 1987 and 3 in 1988 and then was gone. Guerrero and Sax led the offense—if you want to call it that.

# 1988

The one great reason the Dodgers won the pennant and the World Series in 1988 is Orel Hershiser. The Dodgers went from 73 wins to 94. The staff led in complete games (32), shutouts (15) and saves (49). Hershiser won 23 games with an ERA of 2.25. He pitched 267 innings and allowed 90 earned runs. Like Yogi Berra not understanding how Sandy Koufax ever could have lost 5 games in 1964, it's difficult to explain how Orel ever lost 8 games in 1988. He was the dominant hurler on a staff that posted an ERA of 2.96, which goes a long way in explaining its success. But Tim Leary won 17 games, Tim Belcher 12, Holton 7, Pena 6, Jay Howell 5 with 21 saves, Valenzuela 5 and Crews and John Tudor 4 apiece, while Orosco, Hillegas and Don Sutton (who was forty-three years old) won 3 each and Ricky Horton and Ramon Martinez 1 each.

Schenectady, New York native Tudor had won 102 games before he landed with the Dodgers at the end of his career. He was 4-0 the following year and retired. Jesse Orosco has to be truly remarkable. Born in Santa Barbara, California, he lasted 24 seasons in the majors while never winning more than 13 games in any one year. He ended up with 87 wins and 80 losses and a remarkable ERA of 3.16. He pitched with the New York Mets, as well as with Cleveland, Milwaukee, Baltimore, St. Louis and San Diego. He had two stints with the Dodgers: 1988, when he won 3 games, and in 2001–2002, when he collected 1 victory in his second year. Man, these guys can really hold on rather than having to go to work for a living. Steve Sax had 175 hits and Kirk Gibson had 25 homers. Mike Marshall led the team with 82 RBIs. But it was certainly Orel and the dynamic staff that prohibited opponents from scoring that drove the Dodgers to victory.

In the NLCS, Manager Davey Johnson's New York Mets (with Darryl Strawberry, Kevin McReynolds and David Cone) sent the series to a seesaw seven games. The Mets won the first and third games, 3–2 and 8–4, respectively, behind the arm of Randy Myers. Tim Belcher won the second and fifth games for the Dodges, 6–3 and 7–4, and Alejandro Pena got the win in Game 4, 5–4. Cone pitched the Mets to a 5–1 victory in Game 6. In a masterly performance, Hershiser blanked the New Yorkers on five hits in Game 7, 6–0, before a capacity crowd at Dodger Stadium.

This shutout came after Hershiser had pitched 8 innings in Game 1 and 6 innings in Game 3 and earned the save in Game 4. His complete game shutout in the final contest sealed a legendary performance. He had taken the hill in four of the seven games, pitching in many crucial situations, and logged 24 2/3 of a total 65 innings.

Then came the World Series. The Oakland A's were a collection of old and new sluggers—Carney Lansford and Dave Parker, Mark McGwire and Jose Canseco. But the Dodgers provided a lights-out for these guys. Alejandro Pena won Game 1, 5–4, in Los Angeles. Orel prevailed in Game 2, 6–0. Rick Honeycutt, the former Dodger, won the third game for the A's in Oakland, 2–1. Tim Belcher, whose solid postseason was a bit overshadowed by Hershiser's heroics, came back to win the fourth game, 4–3. Orel capped his great season winning the fifth game of the World Series, 5–2, helped by home runs from Mickey Hatcher and Mike Davis. Orel added MVP of the World Series to his Cy Young Award seasons—one of the greatest Dodger seasons ever.

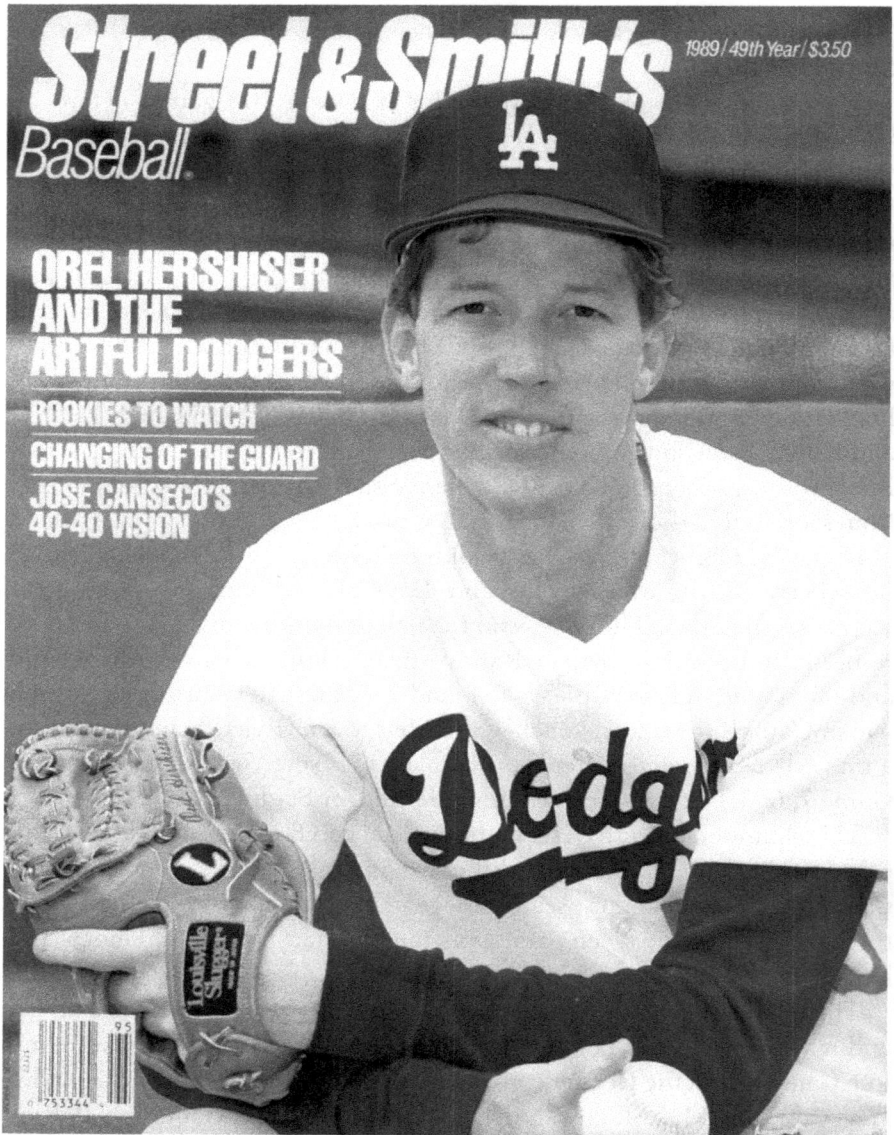

Orel Hershiser experienced one of the greatest pitching years in baseball history in 1988. He won 23 games that year and became the only pitcher to win the Cy Young Award and the Most Valuable Player Award for both the National League Playoffs and the World Series in the same year. *Courtesy of the Sporting News Archives.*

# 1989

The year 1989 was really a weird one for the Dodgers. Their great pitching staff allowed the fewest runs in the league (2.95 ERA), while the offense scored the fewest. They won 77 games. What a team! Hershiser led the pitchers with an ERA of 2.31 and 15 wins, while Belcher also had 15 wins and an ERA of 2.82. Fernando (3.23 ERA) won 10 games, while Mike Morgan (2.53 ERA) won 8, Martinez and Leary 6 apiece, Howell and John Wetteland 5 each, Pena 4 and Ray Searage 3. Searage, from Freeport, New York, spent nine years in the majors and won 11 games. His last two years were with the Dodgers. The anemic offense was led by veteran Eddie Murray's 20 home runs and 88 RBIs. To say that no one else did anything would be an understatement. The great Murray had three good years with the Dodgers, from 1989 to 1991, and then ended his career in L.A. in 1997 at age forty-one. He reached the coveted 500-homer level, finishing with 504, 1,917 RBIs and a batting average of .287 in twenty-one seasons. His fielding percentage at first base was .993—not too shabby.

# The 1990s

The most significant achievement by the Dodgers' staff in the 1990s was that it pitched four no-hitters. Fernando Valenzuela hurled a no-hit game against St. Louis, 6–0, on June 29, 1990. Journeyman Kevin Gross whitewashed San Francisco, 2–0, on August 17, 1992. Ramon Martinez managed a 7–0 no-hitter against the Florida Marlins on July 14, 1995. Hideo Nomo joined them in the exclusive club on September 17, 1996, when twenty-seven Colorado Rockies complied for a 9–0 memory. The only other team to have that many no-hitters in the 1990s was the Yankees. The only 20-game winner of the decade was Ramon Martinez, who went 20-6 in 1990. The decade wasn't the best for ERA, as the team finished with 3.68. The Dodgers did win the Western Division in 1995 but lost the playoff to Cincinnati, 3–0.

The worst thing that happened was the trading of Pedro Martinez in 1992 and catcher Mike Piazza in 1998. These trades were perhaps the two of the greatest blunders in Dodger history, because Pedro won three Cy Young Awards, one in the NL with Montreal and two in the junior circuit with the Boston Red Sox, and Mike became the best-hitting catcher of all time, ending his career with a. 308 average. The Dodgers did win 93 games in 1991, one game behind the division-winning Atlanta Braves, and 90 games in 1996, a game behind San Diego, after the both Major Leagues had gone to three divisions each. The divisions made more geographic sense, as L.A. competed in the four-team NL West with the Giants, Padres and Colorado Rockies.

But that's it for the good seasons. The decade did mark the debut of Hideo Nomo, as he won 16 games in both 1995 and 1996. The arrival of Kevin Brown was auspicious. He was a top talent who won 18 games for the Dodgers in 1999 but soon wore out his welcome.

# 1990

The Dodgers won 86 games in 1990 behind Martinez's 20-win season. Their ERA ballooned to 3.72, seventh in the league, but they did finish number one in complete games with 29. Fernando won 13, Mike Morgan 11, Belcher 9, Mike Hartley 6, Jim Neidinger and Howell 5 apiece, Crews 4, Don Aase and Jim Gott 3 each, Wetteland 2 and 1 apiece for Searage, Dave Walsh, Denny Cook, Hershiser and Terry Wells. Orel pitched in twenty-five innings and tore his rotator cuff on April 25, 1990. He returned to the hill and pitched well thirteen months later, but never with the same dominance.

Mike Hartley came out of Hawthorne, California, and spent three years with the Dodgers, winning 6 and losing 3 in 1990. Neidlinger, of Vallejo, California, spent one year in the majors, starting 12 games in 1990 for the Dodgers and winning 5. Don Aase, from Orange, California, finished his thirteen years in the majors in 1990 with the Dodgers, going 3-1. Dave Walsh, of Arlington, Massachusetts, spent a year in the majors with the Dodgers in 1990, winning 1 game. Denny Cook, of LaMarque, Texas, won 1 game for the Dodgers in both 1990 and 1991, but he spent fifteen seasons in the bigs, winning 64 games. Terry Wells, of Kankakee, Illinois, spent a year in the majors, winning 1 game. Murray hit .330 with 26 home runs, while Kai Daniels had 27.

# 1991

The Dodgers won a whopping 93 games in 1991. Pitching kept them in the lead for a while, pacing the NL in ERA again with 3.06, shutouts (7) and fewest home runs allowed (97). Martinez won 17 games, Morgan 14, Bob

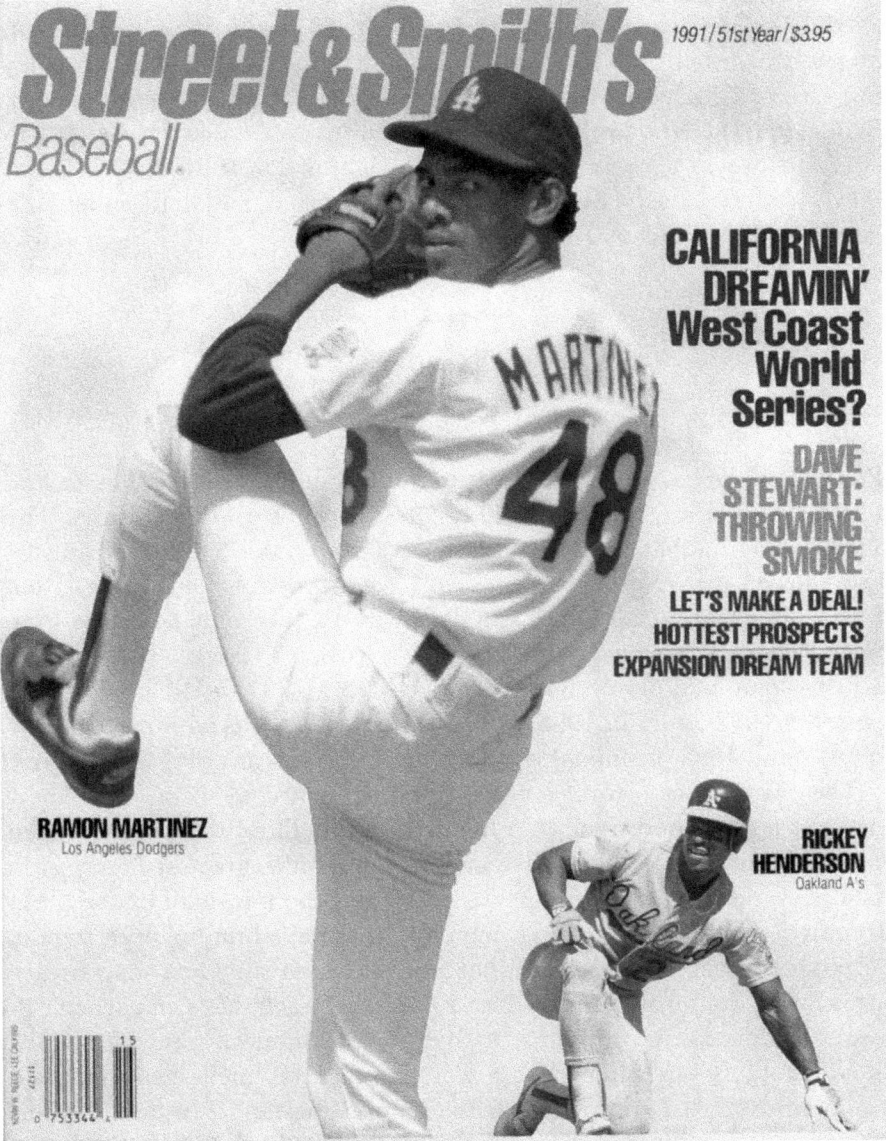

*1991/51st Year/$3.95*

**Street & Smith's**

*Baseball.*

**CALIFORNIA DREAMIN' West Coast World Series?**

**DAVE STEWART: THROWING SMOKE**

**LET'S MAKE A DEAL!**
**HOTTEST PROSPECTS**
**EXPANSION DREAM TEAM**

**RAMON MARTINEZ**
Los Angeles Dodgers

**RICKEY HENDERSON**
Oakland A's

Ramon Martinez went 20-6 in 1990 for the Dodgers with a 2.92 ERA and finished second in the voting for the Cy Young Award. Martinez also pitched a no-hitter in 1995 and won 123 games for the Dodgers. *Courtesy of the Sporting News Archives.*

Ojeda 12, Belcher and Gross 10 each, Hershiser 7 in his comeback season, Roger McDowell and Jay Howell 6 apiece, Jim Gott 4, Mike Hartley and Crews 2 each and Wetteland and John Candelaria 1 victory apiece. Candelaria, the New Yorker who had been the former Pirates ace (20-5 in 1977), spent two years with the Dodgers, winning 2 in 1991 and 1 in 1992. Newly acquired Darryl Strawberry hit 29 home runs, and that was about it except for Brett Butler's 182 hits.

# 1992

The year 1992 was a disaster. To even think about it brings on headaches. The Los Angeles Dodgers lost 99 games, the most in their history. The pitching was not that bad, as the ERA was a respectable 3.41. The Dodgers also allowed the fewest home runs (82). And Gross pitched his no-hitter. Tom Candiotti won 11 games and Orel won 10. The only new guys were Steve Wilson, who won 2 games, and Kip Gross, who won 1. Wilson, from British Columbia, played for the Dodgers from 1991 to 1993, winning 2 games in 1992 and 1 in 1993. Gross, a Nebraskan, was with the Dodgers in 1992 and 1993, winning his only game the first year.

The season was significant only for the arrival of Pedro Martinez, who lost a game and went 10-5 the next year before the Dodgers traded him to Montreal for Delino DeShields, one of the greatest faux pas in major-league history. Martinez was thought to be too small by the great Tommy Lasorda. Way to go, Tommy! So they gave him up, even though he pitched great in 1993. Martinez not only won the Cy Young Award three times, but he also has the best ERA-plus index (that's an earned run average adjusted according to the ballpark) in modern baseball history. Incidentally, Bobby Shantz, who was five feet, six inches and weighed 134 pounds (Pedro grew to five feet, eleven inches and 170 pounds), was 24-7 in 1954 for the Philadelphia Athletics. And Whitey Ford, who topped out at five feet, ten inches and 178 pounds, had the greatest won-lost percentage in baseball history.

# 1993

The pitchers accumulated an ERA of 3.50, good for third place in 1993. The staff was led by Pedro Astacio with 14 wins, followed by Kevin Gross with 13, Orel 12, Pedro Martinez 10, Candiotti 8, McDowell 5, Gott 4, Omar Daal 2 and Wilson, Worrell and Ricky Tricek 1 each. Tricek, from Texas, played a year for the Dodgers and won a game. He pitched five seasons in the majors, winning 5 games. Piazza and Karros were the offensive contributors.

# 1994

The year 1994 was mostly forgettable except for Piazza, who hit 24 homers with 92 RBIs and a .319 batting average in 104 games. The Dodgers won 58 games in a strike-interrupted season. The ERA was a bloated 4.17. The pitching was led by Ramon Martinez with 12 wins. Gross collected 9 and Candiotti 7, while Worrell, Hershiser and Astacio won 6 apiece. Gott managed 5 victories, Ismael Valdes 3, Alfonso Osuna 2 and Rudy Saenz and Gary Wayne 1 each. Saenz, from Brawley, California, pitched two years for the Dodgers, winning 1 game each year. But he pitched seventeen seasons in the bigs, going 41-30 with 13 saves. Osuna, from Inglewood, California, pitched one season for the Dodgers, winning 2 games. Gary Wayne, of Dearborn, Michigan, finished an unremarkable 6 seasons in the majors with 14 victories and a 1-3 record for the Dodgers.

# 1995

The Dodgers won the NL West in 1995 with 78 wins. The staff's ERA of 3.66 was good for second in the league. The playoffs, now best-of-five affairs, included the winners of the East, West and Central Divisions and the best second-place record of the NL division nonwinners. Yet the Dodgers still managed to have to outduel the Cincinnati Reds. Actually, it wasn't really a duel; the Dodgers were swept in three games. Ramon

Hideo Nomo won 81 games for the Dodgers, including a no-hitter in 1998 against the Colorado Rockies. He also became one of only five pitchers in history to throw at least one no-hitter in both leagues. The others are Cy Young, Jim Bunning, Nolan Ryan and Randy Johnson. Nomo hurled his other no-hitter for the Boston Red Sox. *Courtesy of the Sporting News Archives.*

Martinez was 17-7, and Piazza hit .346 with 32 homers. Eric Karros also had 32 home runs and 105 RBIs, and Raul Mondesi hit 26 homers. But the pitching staff also featured Nomo and Valdes, with 13 wins each. Astacio and Candiotti each won 7. Daal, Worrel and Kevin Tapani won 4 each, John Cummings 3, Todd Williams and Antonio Osuna 2 apiece and Felix Rodriguez and Seanez 1 each.

Kevin Tapani, of Des Moines, Iowa, won 143 games in thirteen seasons. He won 4 for the Dodgers that year before moving on. John Cummings, of Torrance, California, pitched two years for the Dodgers, winning 3 in 1995. Todd Williams pitched eight seasons in the majors, winning 12 games. His last year was with the Dodgers, when he won 2. Felix Rodriguez of the Dominican Republic pitched his first year with the Dodgers, winning 1 game. But he lasted another ten seasons, winning 37 games.

# 1996

The Dodgers won a whopping 90 games in 1996 but finished a game behind the division-winning Padres. Still, they made the playoffs as the winningest team among the division nonwinners. Hideo Nomo hurled 16 wins, while Ramon Martinez and Ishmael Valdes each had 15. Osuna, Astacio and Candiotti each won 9, while Scott Radinsky and Chan Ho Park had 5, Worrell 4, Mark Guthrie 2 and Darren Dreifort 1. This was the first of four years with the Dodgers for Guthrie, as he won a total of 5 games. But he hung on in the majors for fifteen seasons, for a 51-54 record with an ERA of 4.05. Piazza continued his great years, batting .336 with 36 homers and 105 RBIs. Eric Karros had 34 homers with 111 RBIs and hit .280.

The Dodgers were blanked once again in the playoffs, swept by the NL East-winning Atlanta Braves, the first team in league history to make five consecutive postseason appearances. This talented group, with Greg Maddux, Tom Glavine, Fred McGriff and Chipper Jones, outscored the L.A. nine, 22–7, with losses distributed to Martinez, Osuna and Nomo.

# 1997

The Dodgers had hitters in 1997, helping muster 88 wins. Piazza hit .362 with 201 hits, 40 homers and 124 RBIs in his greatest year. Three other guys hit more than 30 homers: Karros and Todd Zeile with 31 each, and Raul Mondesi with 30. No one had a lot of wins on the staff, which finished second in ERA (3.62) but had the most shutouts (10) and the most strikeouts (1,232), finishing second in fewest hits allowed (1,325) and second in most innings pitched (1,459). Chan Ho Park and Nomo led with 14 wins each. Martinez, Candiotti and Valdes each won 10, while Astacio won 7, Scott Radinsky and Darren Dreifort 5 apiece, Darren Hall and Osuna 3 each, Dennis Reyes and Todd Worrell 2 each and Mike Harkey, Mark Guthrie and Rick Gorecki 1 each. Reyes pitched two seasons for the Dodgers, winning 2 games, and remarkably is still pitching as this book goes to press: fifteen seasons with 35 wins. Gorecki, of Oak Forest, Illinois, pitched one year for the Dodgers, winning 1 game with an ERA of 15.00. Harkey of San Diego spent eight years in the majors, his last year with the Dodgers.

# 1998

The Dodgers won only 83 in 1998, but the year was notable for two things: the dumping of Piazza and the use of 24 pitchers. The staff with a 3.81 ERA was led by Chan Ho Park, winning 15 games. Ismael Valdez won 11, Dreifort 8 and Antonio Osuna, Dave Milicki and Ramon Martinez 7 apiece. Radinsky won 6, Brian Bohanon 5, Carlos Perez 4 and Jim Bruske 3. Mark Guthrie, Hideo Nomo, Brad Clontz and Eric Weaver won 2 apiece, and Jeff Kubenca and Jeff Shaw won 1 each. Milicki, out of Cleveland, finished 7-3 that year and pitched ten years in the bigs. Brian Bohanon, out of Texas, lasted twelve seasons in the big leagues, if only one year with the Dodgers. He won 54 games. Jim Bruske, who comes from East St. Louis, Illinois, played one year for the Dodgers but lasted five years in the majors with a record of 9-1. Brad Clontz out of Virginia pitched one year for the Dodgers but lasted five years in the majors. Eric Weaver from Springfield, Illinois, pitched three years in the majors, one with the Dodgers. Jeff Kubenca, of

Texas, lasted two years in the bigs, both with the Dodgers. Mondesi hitting 30 homers was the only offense, even though the entire team was offensive, so to speak.

# 1999

In 1999, the Dodgers won 77 games. Eric Gagne, the future of the bullpen, won his first game. This was a spooky year. The team ERA was 4.45, very unfamiliar territory for the Dodgers, and they finished no higher than sixth in any pitching category. Unfortunately, 21 pitchers saw action. Kevin Brown won 18, Park and Dreifort won 13 each and Valdes won 9. Pedro Borbon Jr. won 4, Mike Judd and Alan Mills won 3 apiece and Carlos Perez, Jeff Shaw, Onan Masaoka, Jamie Arnold, Jeff Williams and Robinson Checo each won 2 games. Mike Maddux and Eric Gagne each won 1. Pedro Borbon Jr., from the Dominican Republic, was the son of the great reliever for the Cincinnati Reds; Borbon Jr. went on to pitch nine seasons with 16 wins and 4 saves. Mike Judd, out of San Diego, pitched four seasons with the Dodgers, and this was his best, winning 3.

Alan Mills, out of Florida, pitched two years for the Dodgers, winning 3 games. Jeff Williams, from Australia pitched, four years for L.A., winning 4 games. Checo, of the Dominican Republic, pitched three years in the majors, his last with the Dodgers, winning 2 games. Jamie Arnold, of Dearborn, Michigan, pitched two years for Dodgers, winning 2 games. Onan Masaoka, of Hawaii, was with the Dodgers for two seasons and won 2 games. Mike Maddux, of Dayton, Ohio, pitched fifteen years in the majors, eventually winning 39 games and losing 37. Newly acquired Gary Sheffield hit 34 homers and Mondesi 33.

# The 2000s

The decade of the 2000s had its moments. The team was best known for going through four managers—Davey Johnson, Jim Tracy, Grady Little and former Yankees great Joe Torre. This is the same number of managers the Dodgers employed during the previous four decades—Walt Alston, Tommy Lasorda, Bill Russell and Glenn Hoffman. The owner at the beginning of the decade was the Fox Entertainment Group—basically a division of News Corp., the media conglomerate compiled by Australian tycoon Rupert Murdoch—through 2003, and then it was Frank McCourt from 2004 to 2012.

The Dodgers posted the highest record in the National League West three times. L.A. lost a playoff series to St. Louis in 2004. The Dodgers beat the Chicago Cubs in 2008, only to be defeated by the Phillies for the league pennant. And the Dodgers were back in the fight the next year, taking the Cardinals in the preliminary playoff series but losing again to the Phillies. The team's ERA for the decade was around 4.31, which pretty well says it all. Nobody won 20 games.

The 2000s were significant for two pitchers, Eric Gagne and Clayton Kershaw, and one hitter, Manny Ramirez. Gagne won the Cy Young Award in 2003, posting a record 55 saves and ERA of 1.20. He went on to have 84 saves in a row before his streak was broken. The year 2008 was notable for Kershaw's arrival. He remains a guy who may become one of the best Dodger pitchers ever. Fingers crossed. Big Chan Ho Park won 18 in 2000, Nomo won 16 in 2002 and 2003, and Brad Penny won 16 games in 2006 and

2007. The Bums did win 95 games in 2009 with, believe it or not, twenty-one pitchers gaining wins.

The significant offensive producer in this period was Gary Sheffield, who hit a total of 79 home runs and batted .325 and .311 in 2000 and 2001, respectively. He also knocked in 209 runs and scored 203 before L.A. got rid of him. Shawn Green, Adrian Beltre and Jeff Kent all had their moments and then were gone.

The team highlight of the decade, which lifted blue hopes, was the arrival of Joe Torre, who had managed the Yankees to four World Series victories and then wore out his welcome in New York. Joe was probably the best Dodger manager after Alston and Lasorda. He immediately went to work to win the NL West in both 2008 and 2009, the latter with 95 wins. The volatile Manny Ramirez also came to town and shook up Los Angeles for three years with his dreadlocks, plate expertise and shenanigans off the field.

# 2000

The Bums started off in 2000 winning 86 games. Believe it or not, their collective ERA of 4.10 was second best in the league. The staff also allowed the fewest number of hits, 1,379. Park won 18, Brown 13, Dreifort 12 and Matt Herges 11. Mike Fetters and Terry Adams won 6 each, Carlos Perez 5, Gagne 4, Alan Mills 2 and Onan Masoka, Orel Hershiser and Luke Prokopec 1 each. Fetters won his 6 in the thirteenth year of his career. He won two more the next year. He finished with 100 saves and a 31-41 record with a 3.86 ERA. Prokopec, from Australia, won 1 game in 2000 and a big 8 in 2001. He finished his career in Toronto in 2002. Sheffield had 43 home runs and 109 RBIs, but that didn't seem to help the team much.

# 2001

In 2001, Chan Ho Park led the staff with 15 wins as the Dodgers won 86 games again under new manager Jim Tracy. Terry Adams won 12, Kevin Brown and Matt Herges 9 apiece and Prokopec 8. Gagne, Giovanni and

Carrara won 6 apiece, Dreifort 4 and James Baldwin and Jeff Shaw 3 apiece. Four pitchers won 2: Fetters, Alberto Reyes, Jeff Williams and Andy Ashby. Dennis Springer and Terry Mulholland won 1 apiece. Terry Adams, out of Mobile, Alabama, spent eleven years in the bigs and won 51 games. His second year with the Dodgers was his most prolific. James Baldwin of North Carolina (not the writer) won 3 games in a career in which he won 79 in eleven seasons. Not bad. His ERA was 5.01. Springer, out of Fresno, California, pitched two years for the Dodgers and won 1. Shawn Green was the season's hitting standout, clouting 49 homers and 188 hits for a .297 average.

# 2002

The year 2002 marked the arrival of Eric Gag-Me-with-a-Spoon Gagne (pronounced *gan*-yay, and the betters usually were dispatched to the cheers of the crowd), whose three-year relief run was one of the best in major-league history. The Dodgers won 92 games, and Gagne saved 52 of them with a ERA of .197. Hideo Nomo won 16 games and Odalis Perez 15. Kazuhisa Ishii won 14 and Omar Daal won 11. Ashby won 9 games, Carrara 6, Paul Quantrill and Paul Shuey 5 apiece, Gagne 4, Brown 3 and Guillermo Mota and Jesse Orosco 1 each. Carrara, a Venezuelan native, had two good years with the Dodgers, winning 6 in 2001 and 2002. He pitched ten years in the majors, winning 29 games. Quantrill, out of Canada, pitched two years for the Dodgers, winning 2 games. He hurled fourteen years in the bigs, winning 68 games. Shuey, from Lima, Ohio, pitched two years for the Dodgers, winning 11 games. Shawn Green hit 42 home runs with 114 RBIs.

# 2003

In 2003, Gagne's career peaked with a Cy Young Award and an unbelievable 55 saves with an ERA of 1.20—one of the best years ever by a pitcher. He was lights out, leading the team to 85 victories. Nomo won 16 games, Brown 14, Perez 12, Wilson Alvarez and Mota 6 apiece, Dreifort 4, Ashby 3 and

Gagne, Quantrill, Edwin Jackson and Troy Brohawn 2 apiece. Jackson, out of Georgia, won 2 games each in 2003, 2004 and 2005 for the Dodgers. He went on his way but has never reached expectations, winning 60 big-league games through 2011. Troy Brohawn, of Cambridge, Maryland, won 2 games for the Dodgers and was never heard from again. Hitting stars were virtually absent, with Adrian Beltre belting 23 homers and Green 18.

# 2004

Things brightened up in 2004 with 93 victories and a division title until the Dodgers really found out what it was like to be owned by Frank McCourt. He bought the team financed mostly by debt. How this was ever allowed by Major League Baseball is still a mystery. In 2004, McCourt's South Boston parking lot property was used as collateral for some of the financing to acquire the Dodgers from News Corp. Later, the South Boston property was turned over to News Corp. in exchange for canceling acquisition debt. News Corp. received about $200 million when it resold the property to Morgan Stanley and Boston real estate investor John B. Hynes III in 2006. To finance his purchase, McCourt raised the Dodger Stadium prices of tickets, parking and concessions every year. One of McCourt's brilliant moves was to fire General Manager Dan Evans and hire Paul DePodesta. An advocate of Billy Beane and "small ball," DePodesta traded the team's starting catcher, Paul LoDuca, along with setup pitcher Guillermo Mota and outfielder Juan Encarnacion, for first baseman Hee-Seop Choi, pitcher Brad Penny and pitching prospect Bill Murphy, whose later trade led to the acquisition of veteran Steve Finley. The chubby Choi batted .161 with no homers for the Dodgers, and Finley did hit 13 home runs, but the trade was labeled a big bust because he was on his last legs; Penny did not pitch for a while.

In another brilliant DePodesta move, the Dodgers decided not to sign third baseman Adrian Beltre. That was one of the McCourt era's lousier decisions, since Beltre has hit 132 home runs with 603 RBIs since and has been spectacular in 2010 and 2011 especially. DePodesta did sign J.D. Drew, Derek Lowe and Jeff Kent, all of whom had modest productions for the Dodgers—with Kent eventually becoming an offensive force. Then, at the end of 2005, DePodesta fired one of the better Dodger managers since Lasorda, Jim Tracy, who in 2009 was named National League Manager of the Year for the Colorado Rockies. Shortly after Tracy's firing, McCourt fired DePodesta and brought in Neil Colletti, better if not brilliant. Nobody would mistake him for Branch Rickey. However, Colletti did hire Joe Torre, who had led the Yankees to four World Series triumphs and was a former great National League catcher and infielder—more importantly, he was someone to hearten the fans. Torre proceeded to average 86 wins per year for three years, and the Dodgers were decent if unspectacular.

When the McCourts announced divorce proceedings in October 2009, it was eventually reported that he and his wife, Jamie, had used the Dodgers as their personal ATM, built astronomical debts and even misrepresented a charitable foundation. Eventually, the Dodgers were sold to the Magic Johnson group for $2.15 billion, and unfortunately, McCourt laughed all the way to the bank.

On the field in 2004, the Dodgers actually did a lot better than in the courts and in their financial dealings. The team ERA was a mediocre 4.01, but the Dodgers won 93 games and a division title under manager Jim Tracy. Jose Lima led the staff with a 13-5 record. Weaver won 13, and so did Ishii. Mota gathered 8 victories and Gagne and Alvarez 7 each. This was followed by Yhency Brazoban with 6, Carrara 5, Nomo 4, Duaner Sanchez 3, Jackson 2 and Elmer Dessens, Brian Falkenborg, Brad Penny and Dreifort with 1 each. Brazoban, of the Dominican Republic, pitched from 2004 to 2008 with L.A. and won 10 games. Dessens, from Mexico, pitched three years for the Dodgers, winning 2 games. Falkenborg, from Newport Beach, pitched three years for L.A., winning 2 games. Duaner Sanchez of Mexico pitched two years for the Dodgers, winning 3 in 2004 and 4 in 2005. The playoff loss to St. Louis sealed the season.

# 2005

In 2005, the Dodgers sank to 71 wins with a terrible ERA of 4.38. Weaver was 14-11 and Derek Lowe 12-15. Penny, Perez and Carrara won 7 each, D.J. Houlton 6 and Yhency Brazoban and Duaner Sanchez 4 each. Steve Schmoll and Edwin Jackson won 2 apiece, and Wilson Alvarez, Jonathan Broxton and Eric Gagne won 1 each. The hitters were led by Jeff Kent with 29 home runs and 105 RBIs. Schmoll, of Silver Spring, Maryland, pitched one year in the bigs, going 2-2 for the Dodgers.

# 2006

In 2006, veteran Grady Little took over as manager, and the Dodgers managed to win 88 games. The staff had the most complete games (15) and allowed the fewest home runs (152). The pitching was led by Lowe and Penny, each with 16 wins. Aaron Sele and Brett Tomko won 8 apiece and Chad Billingsley 7. Takashi Saito posted 24 saves, and former Atlanta Brave great and future Hall of Famer Greg Maddux went 6-3. Danys Baez won 5, Jonathan Broxton and Odalis Perez 4 apiece and Hendrickson, Joe Beimel and Jae Weong Seo won 2 each. Hong-Chi Kuo and Eric Stults each had 1 victory.

Aaron Sele, from Golden Valley, Minnesota, won 148 games in the bigs in fifteen seasons but only those 8 in one year with the Dodgers. Brett Tomko, of Cleveland, Ohio, pitched two seasons for the Dodgers, winning 8 games. Danys Baez, out of Cuba and in his tenth season, won 5 games that year. Overall, he lasted fourteen seasons with 100 wins. Mark Hendrickson of Mount Vernon, Washington, won 2 games for the Dodgers in 2006 and 4 in 2007. Seo, a South Korean, was 2-4 for the Dodgers and pitched his last year in 2007, for a total of six seasons, winning 28 games. Eric Stults, from Plymouth, Indiana, won 1 game in 2006 and a total of 8 through 2009. Rafael Furcal collected 196 hits and batted an even .300. J.D. Drew and Nomar Garciaparra each hit 20 homers. Nobody else did much.

# 2007

In 2007, the Dodgers won 82 games, with Brad Penny winning 16 and Lowe and Billingsley 12 each, Randy Wolf 9, Rudy Saenz 6 and Broxton, Beimel, Hendrickson and David Wells 4 apiece. Scott Proctor won 3, and Tomko and Saito 2 apiece, with latter accruing an impressive 39 saves. Stults, Kuo, Jason Schmidt and Esteban Loaiza all won 1 each. Proctor, who has pitched nine years in the bigs, was 3-0 in 2007 and 2-0 in 2008. He signed with a Korean team for the 2012 season. Jason Schmidt had won 71 games the previous five years for San Francisco and came to the Dodgers, but injuries reduced him to 1 win in 2007 and 2 in 2008, and he made his exit from baseball. Kuo had his one great year. Loaiza went 1-4 in 2007 for the Dodgers and 1-2 in 2008.

He was on the end of a fourteen-year career, in which he won 126 games, including 21 with the Chicago White Sox in 2003. Juan Pierre had 196 hits, but the Dodgers never acted like they respected him.

# 2008

The 2008 Dodgers featured more mediocrity, but the Dodgers won the division title and beat the Chicago Cubs before losing to the Phillies in the National League playoffs. They only won 84 games (six more than they lost), but the pitching staff did a lot better. The guys had the best team ERA (3.68) again and also finished number one in fewest home runs (123) allowed. Billingsley won 16 and Lowe 14. Kuroda won 9, Penny 6, Kershaw and Kuo 5 apiece, Saito (18 saves) and Park 4 each and Broxton 3, while Maddux, Stults, Proctor and Falkenborg won 2 apiece and Troncoso, Jason Johnson and Loaiza won 1 each. Ramon Troncoso, from the Dominican Republic, went 1-1 for the Dodgers in 2008, 5-4 in 2009 and 2-3 in 2010. He didn't get a decision in 2011 but pitched 22.2 innings. Jason Johnson of Santa Barbara pitched eleven seasons in the majors, winning 50 games, but he only pitched one year for the Dodgers, winning one game. Manny Ramirez, a crowd favorite, lit the stadium afire. He hit .396 with 17 home runs and 53 RBIs in as many games.

To say that the Dodgers overwhelmed the Cubs in the divisional playoffs would be an understatement. The Cubs had won 97 games, the most in the National League, and the Dodgers blew them away. Manny hit three home runs, and Lowe won the first game, 7–2, Billingsley the second, 10–3, and Kuroda the third. The NL pennant series was another story, as the Phillies won four out of five. Lowe did all right in the first game, losing 3–2, and Kuroda won the third game, 7–2. Otherwise, the Dodgers were inert.

# 2009

In 2009, the Dodgers won an incredible 95 games and back-to-back division titles. Twenty-two pitchers won at least one game. It probably helped that the team ERA was 3.40, as they finished first again. They also finished first in fewest hits (1,265) allowed and second in most strikeouts (1,272). Billingsley won 12 games. Randy Wolf had 11, and Jonathan Broxton posted an impressive 36 saves and 7 wins. Of the rest of team, Kershaw and Kuroda collected 8 wins, Jeff Weaver 6 and Troncosa and James McDonald 5 apiece, while Ronald Belisario, Eric Stults and Vicente Padilla won 4 each. Guillermo Mota and Jon Garland won 3 apiece, while Cory Wade, Eric Milton, Brent Leach, Kuo, Scott Elbert and Jason Schmidt all won 2. George Sherrill, Charlie Haeger and Will Ohman won 1 apiece. Whew! McDonald, of Long Beach, won 5 games in three years with the Dodgers. He went to Pittsburgh to reveal some of the prowess the Dodgers thought he had. Belisario, of Venezuela, pitched three years with the Dodgers and won 5 games. Eric Milton, from State College, Pennsylvania, who won 89 games in the bigs, finished off with the Dodgers with 2 wins. Brent Leach, out of Mississippi, played one season in the bigs and won 2 games for the Dodgers. George Sherrill, from Memphis, Tennessee, played two years for the Dodgers and won 3 games each. Charlie Hager, of Livonia, Mississippi, pitched one year for the Dodgers, winning this lone game. Will Ohman, who attended Pepperdine University in Malibu, California, spent one season with the Dodgers, winning 1 game.

The Dodgers bested the St. Louis Cardinals in a three-game sweep as Jeff Weaver won the first game, 5–3. George Sherill won the second game, 3–2, and Padilla got the third win, 5-1, when veteran Mark Loretta hit a game-ending single to score Casey Blake.

The playoff for the championship was a different story. The Phillies won, four games to one, with only Padilla, matched against Pedro Martinez, winning, 2–1, in Game 1. The team batting average for the year was .270, with solid performances by Matt Kemp, who hit .297 with 26 home runs and 101 RBIs, and Andre Ethier, who had 31 home runs and 106 RBIs.

# The 2010s

O f course, the most monumental event of this decade—so far—is
the departure of Frank McCourt and the arrival of Magic Johnson
and friends. But something else remarkable happened in 2011. Clay
Kershaw, at twenty-three, won the Triple Crown of pitching by leading
the National League in wins (21), ERA (2.28) and strikeouts (248) in 2011.
Centerfielder Matt Kemp, twenty-seven, came into his own and flirted
with batting's Triple Crown, leading the NL with 39 home runs and 126
RBIs and placing third in batting with a .324 average. He should have
won MVP but finished second to Ryan Braun and the more successful
Milwaukee Braves.

Manager Joe Torre decided to retire at the end of 2010, and Don
Mattingly, another former Yankee, took over as manager in 2011. Torre,
who had great success managing the Yankees, had spent his entire playing
career in the National League with the Braves, Cardinals and Mets.
Mattingly was great at the plate, finishing his fourteen-year career with
a .307 average, 222 homeruns and 1,099 RBIs. He also was a great first
baseman and finished with a .996 fielding average. Yankee hate abates
for defectors.

# 2010

In 2010, it was back to normal for the mighty Dodgers as they won 80 games. The pitching was lackluster except for Kershaw, as the team ERA was a mediocre 4.01. Kershaw was 13-10 with a 2.91 ERA. He had to be one of the greatest Dodger discoveries of the last 30 years. If Kershaw does not prove to be one of the L.A.'s greatest pitchers, it will be a surprise to many of us. Billingsley won 12 and Kuroda 11. Newly acquired Lilly won 7, Padilla 6, Broxton and Weaver 5 apiece, John Ely 4 and Kuo, Belisario and Carlos Monasterios 3 apiece. Troncoso and George Sherrill won 2 each, and Ramon Ortiz, Kenley Jansen, Travis Schlichting and Octavio Dotel each won a game. It took seventeen pitchers to win 80 games.

John Ely hails from Harvey, Illinois, and he pitched two years for the Dodgers, going 4-10 in 2010 and 0-1 in 2011. He was drafted by the Chicago White Sox in 2007 out of the University of Miami and made his debut with the Dodgers in 2010. He won 3 of his first 4 decisions and struggled the rest of the way, losing 9 times. He was outrighted to the minors in November 2011. Monasterios, from Venezuela, pitched 88.1 innings in 2010 to finish with a 3-5 record and a 4.38 ERA. But he injured his arm, and in the fall of 2011 he was also outrighted to the minors. Kenley Jansen, from Curacao, on the Dodger forty-man roster of 2012, was 1-0 in 2010 and 2-1 in 2011. Schlichting was 1-0 for the Dodgers in 2010 and wasn't on the forty-man roster in 2012. Dotel has been in the bigs for thirteen years and was 1-1 for the Dodgers in 2010. He signed a one-year contract with Toronto for 2012. The hitters were led by Loney, Kemp and Ethier.

# 2011

Kershaw's mindboggling year of 2011 was aided by Kuroda with 13 wins, Ted Lilly with 12 and Chad Billingsley with 11. The team ended up with 82 wins—not too great, considering the years that Kershaw and center fielder Matt Kemp had. Also winning games were Matt Guerrier and Rubby De La Rosa with 4, Mike MacDougal and Dana Eveland with 3 and Javy Guerra, Kenley Jansen and Blake Hawksworth with 2 each. Jon Garland, Nathan Eovaldi, Josh Lindblom, Hong-Chi Kuo and Broxton all won 1. De

La Rosas was a hotshot from the Dominican Republic in his first year, and he was on the forty-man roster in the spring of 2012. Mike MacDougal, from Wake Forest University, spent eleven years in the bigs before coming to the Dodgers in 2011, and he was on the spring roster. Dana Eveland, from California, spent six years in the majors before coming to the Dodgers. He has won 19 games. Javy Guerra, from Denton, Texas; Hawksworth, from Canada; Eovaldi, from Alvin, Texas; and Josh Lindbloom, from Indiana, all spent their first year in the majors with L.A.

That brings us to 2012, when the Dodgers were the best team in baseball for almost three months thanks to timely hitting and fine pitching, as well as the presence of Matt Kemp and Andre Ethier. Newcomer Chris Capuano was 9-2 after the first 75 games and Ted Lilly 5-1. Kershaw had a fine 2.65 ERA but was only 6-4, thanks to some shoddy support. Kemp was phenomenal leading the majors at times in batting average, RBIs and home runs. But because of a severe hamstring injury, he only played in 36 of the first 75 games. He hit .355 with 12 home runs and 28 RBIs in 36 games. Not bad. Meanwhile, Ethier was going through a slump but was second in the National League with 55 RBIs and was hitting .294 with 10 home runs. But it was the rest of the team of unheralded players like Jerry Hairston Jr., A.J. Ellis, Tony Gwynn Jr. and veteran Bobby Abreu, as well as pitchers like Aaron Harang (5 wins), Chad Billingsley and Kenley Jansen (4 wins each), that helped hold the team together. Other pitchers like Josh Lindbloom, Nathan Eovoldi, Jamey Wright and Ronald Belisario also had their moments.

Unfortunately, reality started to set in and by the end of June, the Dodgers had lost their great lead and were sitting at 43-31, only two games ahead of the San Francisco Giants. The basic problems were their offense and having many unproven pitchers. Without Kemp and also injured second baseman Mark Ellis, the Dodgers stumbled badly in June, winning 11 and losing 12 as of June 24. The future depended on the bats of Kemp and Ethier and the arms of Kershaw and hurlers who needed to show they could be part of the legacy of one of the greatest pitching franchises in major-league history. When you read this, the season will be over. Are they part of that legacy?

# Ranking of Los Angeles Dodger Starting Pitchers

The Top 50 Dodger starting pitchers are profiled here, descending from No. 50. The bold line indicates the rank of the subject in Dodgers history as selected by the author, whether he threw right-handed (RP) or left (LP), his years with Los Angeles and his overall won-lost record with L.A.

**50. Bob Ojeda, LP (1991–92), 18-18**. Ojeda is best known for the great 18-5 year (2.57 ERA) he had with the 1986 World Series–winning New York Mets. Ojeda also was the only survivor of the 1993 boating accident that took the lives of fellow Cleveland Indians pitchers Tim Crews (the former Dodger) and Steve Olin. Ojeda, who attended College of the Sequoias in Visalia, was drafted by the Boston Red Sox in 1978. He pitched for Boston and the Mets before coming to the Dodgers and posting a 12-9 record in 1991 and a 6-9 mark in 1992. His ERA was 3.40 with the Dodgers. He won an important game in the pennant race in 1991. Ojeda, who retired in 1994, is a studio analyst for Mets broadcasts.

**49. Guillermo Mota, RP (2002–4, 2009), 18-14**. Mota, at a rangy six feet, six inches and 240 pounds, was born in 1973 in the Dominican Republic and was pitching for the San Francisco Giants as this book went to press. He came to the Dodgers in 2002. Mota originally signed in 1990 as an infielder by the New York Mets. He was taken by the Montreal Expos in a special draft in 1996 and converted to a pitcher. He pitched in his first game in 1999 and came to the Dodgers in 2002. In his best year, Mota went 8-4 for the

Dodgers in 2004. Boasting an 18-14 overall record with the Dodgers, Mota posted a great ERA of 2.79 with the Dodgers and averaged 7.2 strikeouts per game. He's still pitching and will be thirty-nine in July 2012.

**48. Ted Lilly, LP (2010–2011), 19-18**. Lilly, who was born in Torrance, California, and raised in Oakhurst, California, was drafted by the Dodgers in 1996 and traded to Montreal the same year. He has pitched in the majors for thirteen years (2012 marked his fourteenth) and had eight years in a row of double-digit wins with Oakland, Toronto and the Chicago Cubs before coming to the Dodgers in 2010. Lilly posted a 7-4 record with the Dodgers in 2010 and 12-14 in 2011. Lilly's ERA was 3.86, and he averaged 7.8 strikeouts per game and only 2.2 walks. If he continues pitching and winning for the Dodgers, he would move up this list—at least figuratively.

**47. Matt Herges, RP (1999–2001), 20-13**. Herges, from Champaign, Illinois, graduated from Illinois State University and was signed by the Dodgers in 1992. He made his debut with the Dodgers in 1999 at age twenty-nine and had a brilliant next year. In 2000, he ended up 11-3 with an ERA of 3.17. Herges went on to pitch eleven years in the majors for Montreal, San Diego, San Francisco, Arizona, Florida, Colorado and Cleveland—a journeyman, but a good one. His ERA with the Dodgers was a fine 3.38.

**46. Randy Wolf, LP (2007, 2009), 20-13**. A native of Canoga Park, California, Wolf was an all-American at Pepperdine University and was drafted by the Dodgers in 1994 but did not sign. He eventually signed with the Philadelphia Phillies in 1997 and started pitching in the majors in 1999. He came to the Dodgers in 2007, went 9-6 and returned to the team in 2009 and went 11-7. His ERA was 3.72, with 2.8 walks per game. He was pitching for the Milwaukee Brewers at press time.

**45. Antonio Osuna, RP (1995–2000), 24-21**. Antonio came out of Mexico in 1995 and pitched six years for the Dodgers, winning 24 games and losing 21 with an ERA of 3.28 and 9.6 strikeouts per 9 innings. Geez, that's better than Koufax, but Sandy only pitched 1,900 innings more. Osuna never won more than 9 games (1996) with the Dodgers and lasted eleven seasons in the bigs. Even though he was only five feet, eleven inches and 160 pounds, Osuna was a hard thrower and posted consecutive ERAs of 3.00, 2.19 and 3.06 with the Dodgers. He also pitched for the Chicago White Sox, San Diego Padres, New York Yankees and Washington Nationals. His last year in baseball in the Major Leagues was 2005, and his lifetime ERA is 3.68. Osuna jointed the Tires de Quintana Roo in 2007, had a 1.61 ERA in twenty-two games and was on the all-star team. He played again in 2008 but had an ERA of 7.94. He and his wife, Arcelia, have three children: Yohami, Lenix and Yorvit. His sixteen-year-old nephew was signed by the Toronto Blue Jays in 2011.

**44. Rick Sutcliffe, RP (1976–81), 22-21**. Rick Sutcliffe, from Kansas City, Missouri, became a front-rank pitcher in the Major Leagues for eighteen seasons, winning 171 games and chalking up 14 or more wins ten times. Big Rick was six feet, seven inches and 215 pounds, and he pitched for the Dodgers from age twenty to twenty-five (five seasons), racking up 23 wins against 21 losses. In fact, he won 17 games in 1979, which was officially his first year, winning NL Rookie of the Year, the first of four Dodgers to win the award consecutively. But Rick was just getting started. He was 17-10 for the Dodgers in 1979, but they let him get away. In one of their brilliant moves (detect heavy sarcasm here), they traded him to the Cleveland Indians for journeyman outfield Jorge Orta, who played one year for the Dodgers, hitting a monumental .217. Sutcliffe, the "Red Baron" (he had blazingly red hair and a red beard), accented his career with an enormous 16-1 season for the Chicago Cubs in 1984, winning the Cy Young Award. He had 155 strikeouts and thirty-nine walks that year.

**43. Pete Mikkelson, RP (1969–72), 24-17**. Mikkelson won a grand total of 24 games for the Dodgers, but he also saved 20. Pete, who came out of Alhambra, California, in 1964 at the age of twenty-four, pitched for the New York Yankees, Pittsburgh, Chicago Cubs and St. Louis before coming to the Dodgers in 1968. His lifetime ERA for nine seasons was 3.38. Pitching for the Yanks, he is most famous for giving up a three-run homer to Tim McCarver of St. Louis in the tenth inning of Game 5 of the 1964 World Series. It cost New York the game and ultimately the series. His best year was 1967 with the Pirates, posting a 3.07 ERA, winning 9 games and saving 14. He had productive years for the Dodgers from 1969 to 1972, winning 24 and posting an ERA of 2.77 and 2.76 in 1969 and 1970. Pete died in 2006 in Mabton, Washington, at the age of sixty-seven.

**42. Joe Moeller, RP (1962–71), 26-36**. Joe Moeller came out of Mira Costa High School in Manhattan Beach, California. Big things were always expected of Joe, who was six feet, five inches and became the L.A. Dodgers'

Pete Mikkelson, out of Staten Island, New York, won 24 games in his four years with the Dodgers, but he had an excellent ERA of 3.00. Pete, who also pitched for the Yankees, Pirates, Cubs and Cardinals, died in the state of Washington in 2006 at the age of sixty-seven. *Courtesy of the Los Angeles Dodgers.*

youngest starting pitcher at nineteen years and two months. But Joe delivered infrequently. He won 26 games for the Dodgers in eight seasons. He lost 36 games and had an ERA of 4.01. His best season was in 1964, when he won 7 games. He was on the roster for the 1966 World Series team and pitched two innings, allowing a hit. He has been an advance scout for the Florida Marlins since 2002.

**41. Tim Leary, RP (1987–89), 26-29**. Tim Leary was a hard-throwing six-foot, three-inch specimen out of Santa Monica High School who won 26 games for the Dodgers. Leary pitched from 1987 to 1989, but he had a really big year in 1988, when he won 17 games and helped the Dodgers win the pennant. He had an ERA of 2.91 for the year and 1.35 in the World Series, in which the Dodgers beat the favored Oakland A's 4 games to 2. Leary pitched thirteen years in the bigs, retiring in 1994. He won 78 games and lost 105 with an ERA of 4.26, keeping a hill-staff job for thirteen years.

**40. Roger Craig, RP (1958–61), 26-15**. Roger Craig will always be a great name in Dodger history, even though he only played seven years for them. He came up in 1955 to help the Brooklyn Dodgers win the pennant with a 5-3 record. Craig, at six feet, four inches and 185 pounds, was born in 1930 in Durham, North Carolina, and mastered the split-finger fastball. Craig started two games in the 1959 World Series for the Dodgers, won 74 and lost 98 during his twelve seasons, with a respectable 3.83 ERA. He started four games in the World Series for the Dodgers in Brooklyn and L.A., and he relieved in two for the St. Louis Cardinals, as his teams won three out of the four World Series in which he pitched. Craig retired in 1966 and managed the San Francisco Giants, for whom his record was 72-90.

**39. Bob Miller, RP (1963–67), 29-33**. Bob Miller pitched for the Dodgers during the Koufax era but later was a much-traveled hurler. He ended up pitching seventeen years in the majors with a lifetime ERA of 3.37, which is what kept up his value, with ten different teams. He won 69 games over that span, 29 of them for the Dodgers. He was a reliable part of L.A.'s pennant-winning Koufax years. Bob was born in St. Louis and was a star pitcher in high school before signing with the Cardinals. He spent four years with St. Louis and one with the hapless Mets, for whom he went 1-12, before joining the Dodgers staff. He had four straight years where his ERA was 2.89, 2.62, 2.97 and 2.77. His best year was 1963 when he went 10-8. He never won a lot of games, but he hung on for an incredible seventeen years, so his lifetime

Joe Moeller, a local boy from Manhattan Beach, California, is best known for pitching during the Dodger glory years, from 1962 to 1966. He pitched his entire big-league career for the Dodgers. *Courtesy of the Los Angeles Dodgers.*

ERA of 3.37 had to have something to do with it. Roberto Clemente once claimed that Miller was the most difficult pitcher for him to hit against. Miller died of injuries he suffered in an auto accident in Rancho Bernardo, California, in 1993. He had spent several years as a minor-league manager and big-league pitching coach.

**38. Alejandro Pena, RP (1981–89), 38-38**. Pena, born in the Dominican Republic in 1959, made his debut in 1981 with the Dodgers, with whom he played for nine years. His best years were 1993 and 1994, when he won 12 games each season. And he had a great ERA of 2.92. Pena's best year was probably 1991, when he was traded to the Atlanta Braves and went 13 for 13 in saves to help the Braves win the pennant. He ended up with a 56-52 record and a lifetime ERA of 3.11, pitching with six different teams. In 1991, Pena combined with Brave pitchers Kent Mercker and Mark Wohlers for a 1-0 no-hitter against the Padres.

**37. Mike Morgan, RP (1989–91), 33-36**. Morgan was six feet, three inches and 190 pounds, and he played twenty-two seasons, winning 149 games. A high school player from Las Vegas, he once won 16 games in a season, with the Chicago Cubs in 1992. He won 13 in 1999 with Texas. His lifetime ERA was 4.53. He played three seasons with the Dodgers, winning 8, 11 and 14 games, respectively. His earned run average was an impressive 2.78 in 1991. He played for thirteen teams and is only one of twenty-nine players to have played in four decades. Mike was drafted by the Oakland A's in the first round in 1978. He came to the Dodgers in 1989 for center fielder Mike Devereaux. He made the NL All-Star Team in 1991 with his 14-10 mark. Morgan lives in Ogden, Utah, and runs World Championship Outfitters, a private hunting business. He also instructs youth baseball players one on one and became a volunteer coach with a high school in Pleasant Grove, Utah. He also created Robinson's Transport Wounded Warrior Hunt, searching out former military personnel who have received the Purple Heart. Quite a guy.

**36. Kazuhisa Ishii, LP (2002–4), 36-25**. Kazuhisa was born in Japan in 1973 and started playing pro ball at the age of eighteen. He pitched for ten years in Japan before he was signed by the Dodgers in 2002. He won 14, 9 and 13 games, respectively, in his three years. His biggest problem was his control, as he averaged 5.8 walks per game. Then he went to the Mets, for whom he won only 3 games, so he returned to Japan. Ishii was a very important

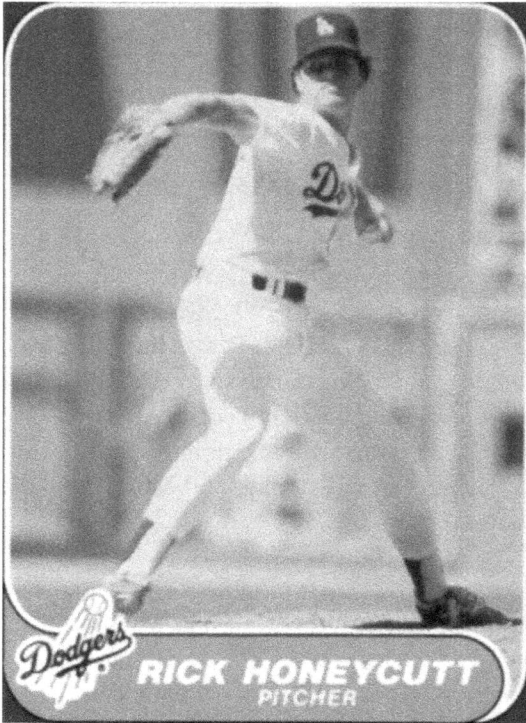

Rick Honeycutt won 33 games with the Dodgers. His best years with L.A. were in 1986 and 1984, when he won 11 and 10 games, respectively. He won 109 games in twenty-one years in the Major Leagues. *Courtesy of Upper Deck.*

member of the Dodgers the years he was there. He is back pitching in Japan. Known for his wit, he often told newspaperman he was sorry for not being funny enough.

**35. Rick Honeycutt, LP (1983–87), 33-42.** Rick Honeycutt pitched for the Dodgers from 1983 to 1987, winning 33 games. He had pretty good years in 1983 and 1984, winning 10 and 11 games, respectively. Rick, who was born in Chattanooga, Tennessee, in 1954, had quite a long career, pitching a whopping twenty-one years in the bigs for six different teams, winning 109 games, with 38 saves. His ERA with the Dodgers was 3.60, but he had a knack for coming through in big games. That's probably why he has been pitching coach for the Dodgers since 2007. He had a pretty phenomenal career for someone who never won more than 14 games (1983) in one season. He made 268 starts, with 529 relief appearances. He was a setup man in Oakland, very successfully, from 1988 to 1993.

**34. Jeff Weaver, RP (2004–5, 2009–2010), 38-29.** Jeff was born in Northridge, California, in 1956 and had two solid seasons for the Dodgers, winning 27 games. He returned to the Dodgers in 2009 and 2010 and won another 11 games. He finished with 38 wins and 29 losses for the Dodgers, with an ERA of 4.21. He retired after the 2010 season.

**33. Kevin Gross, RP (1991–94), 40-44.** Gross, who was born in Downey, California, in 1961, played only four years for the Dodgers but won 40 games. He pitched 678 innings and posted an ERA of 3.63. Kevin, who signed first with the Phillies, had won 80 games before he came to the Dodgers in 1991. He then pitched for Texas and the Anaheim Angels before retiring. He ended up winning 142 wins in fifteen seasons, posting nearly 9 wins per season.

**32. Hiroki Kuroda, RP (2008–2011), 41-46.** Kuroda, who was thirty-five in 2010, came to the Dodgers from Japan in 2008. It's too bad he couldn't have spent his entire career with the Dodgers, but his savvy has stood him in good stead. He was 41-46 with the Dodgers with an ERA of 3.45 and only 2.1 walks per nine innings through 2011. The son of a professional baseball player, Kuroda won more than 100 games in Japan before coming to the United States. He signed with the Yankees for about $10 million for 2012.

**31. Odalis Perez, LP (2002–6), 45-40.** Hailing from the Dominican Republic, Perez spent five years with the Dodgers, going 45-40 with an ERA of 3.94. Perez demonstrated great control, only walking two per nine innings. Born in 1977, Perez was signed by the Atlanta Braves in 1998, pitching three years for them before coming to the Dodgers. He pitched for Kansas City in 2006 and 2007 and for Washington in 2008 before retiring. Perez lasted ten seasons in the bigs, with four teams, winning 73 and losing 82. He was the first Dodger lefty to have 12 wins two seasons in a row since Fernando Valenzuela. Perez was also one of the majors' leading strikeout pitchers. In August 2002, he pitched eight scoreless innings against the Arizona Diamondbacks and slugged his first career home run to win the game 1-0. He became the first big-league pitcher to win a 1-0 game and hit the game-winning homer since Bob Welch of the Dodgers did the same thing on June 17, 1983. This game also began Eric Gagne's streak of 84 consecutive saves.

**30. Darren Dreifort, RP (1994–2004), 48-60.** Dreifort was one of the Dodgers' biggest disappointments—to himself and the team, mostly due to injuries. He was always touted for big things, and he did manage to win 48 games for the Dodgers. Born in Wichita, Kansas, in 1972, Dreifort was drafted in 1980 by the New York Mets. Instead, he attended Wichita State University, where eventually he was the named the NCAA Player of the Year. He was drafted in the first round—second after Alex Rodriguez—by the Dodgers. He is one of a few major-league pitchers who made their debut without ever pitching in the minor leagues. He missed the 1995 season due to injuries and returned for the 1996 and 1997 seasons, pitching effectively as a setup man. He got his first career win in 1996 in relief against the Phillies. He had a very good year in 1997, finishing 5-2 with a 2.86 ERA and 4 saves. He made his first start in April 1998 against the Houston Astros. He won 8 games in 1998, 13 in 1999 and 12 in 2000.

In 2001, super agent Scott Boras convinced the Dodgers to give him a five-year $55 million contract in spite of his unspectacular record and arm trouble. He pitched only 204 more innings in three years, winning 9 games. In Dreifort's first year of the new deal, he had elbow reconstruction surgery in early July, which kept him out until the end of 2002. With continuing arm and shoulder trouble, plus additional knee and hip trouble, Dreifort actually pitched in only three of the five years of the deal, missing the entire 2005 season and parts of two other seasons during that time. Dreifort apparently had a degenerative condition that weakened his connective tissues, as well as a deformed femur. He reportedly had twenty surgeries during his career. Dreifort retired in 2004 at age thirty-two. Divorced with three sons, he lives in Pacific Palisades and is a Dodger minor-league spring training instructor. He was inducted into the College Baseball Hall of Fame in 2009.

**29. Pedro Astacio**, **RP (1992–97), 48-47**. Astacio won 48 games for the Dodgers but also lost 47. Born in the Dominican Republic in 1968, he was signed by the Dodgers in 1992 at age twenty-three. He pitched six years for the Dodgers, with his best year coming in 1993, when he was 14-9. Astacio went on to pitch for Colorado, Houston, Boston, Texas, the New York Mets, San Diego and Washington, winning 129 games in fifteen seasons for an average of 9 wins per season. His best season was 1999 in Colorado, when he won 17 games. He did not officially retire but has not pitched in the majors since 2007.

**28. Rick Rhoden**, **RP (1974–78), 42-24**. Rhoden is quite remarkable. He was born in Florida in 1953 and suffered from osteomyelitis as a boy, wearing a brace until he was twelve years old. That didn't stop him any. He went on to be a star pitcher in high school and then play in the minor leagues until the Dodgers signed him in 1974. Rhoden won 42 games for the Dodgers and only lost 24 for a .636 percentage with an ERA of 3.40. He went on to pitch sixteen years in the majors, mostly with Pittsburgh, where he won 79 games. But he also won 28 games with the Mets over two seasons, 1988 and 1989. Rhoden won 151 games with an ERA of 3.59. After baseball, he wasn't through with sports. He went on to become a pro golfer and has done quite well. He has continued to compete in tournaments as he nears sixty. He won the American Century Celebrity Golf Classic eight times, making him one of the top two-sport athletes.

**27. Al Downing, LP (1971–77), 46-47**. "Gentleman Al" did a good job for the Dodgers. Born in 1941 in Trenton, New Jersey, Al signed with the Yankees in 1961. He pitched nine years for the Yankees and finished 72-57. Downing led the AL in strikeouts in 1964 with 217. He was traded to Oakland and then to Milwaukee before settling with the Dodgers in 1971. He had a great year, winning 20 games, and went on to be named the Comeback Player of the Year. He had 5 shutouts and finished third in the Cy Young Award balloting. Al finished 46-37 with the Dodgers in seven years, and his ERA was 3.16. He won 6.6 games per year. He is probably best known for giving up Hank Aaron's 715th home run to break Babe Ruth's record on April 8, 1974. Downing was a sports talk show host for the Dodgers for a time and remains with the Dodgers' Speaker's Bureau.

**26. Charlie Hough, RP (1970–80), 47-46**. Charlie was a character and a competitor. He was signed out of Hialeah High School in Honolulu, Hawaii. After playing three years in the minors, he developed a knuckleball and played for the Dodgers for eleven years, winning 47 and losing 46, with 60 saves. Charlie went on to play a remarkable twenty-five years in the majors, posting an exact .500 record, winning 216 and losing 216. He was in double figures in wins and losses for the Texas Rangers from 1982 through 1990. He pitched until he was forty-six years old! You have to like a guy like that. His ERA was 3.50 with the Dodgers and 3.75 for twenty-five years. That ain't hay. He has been a pitching coach for a variety of teams.

**25. Tim Belcher, RP (1987–91), 50-38**. Timmy Belcher won 50 games for the Dodgers and only lost 38, which is pretty good. He had an ERA of 2.99, which is great. Born in Ohio in 1961, Belcher played college ball before being drafted by the Minnesota Twins in 1983, coming to the Dodgers in 1987. He stayed in L.A. to post 50 wins in five years. Belcher won 146 games in fourteen seasons in the bigs, for seven different clubs. His best years were the three he spent with Kansas City, for which he won a total of 42 games. He retired in 2001 and has been working as pitching coach for the Cleveland Indians.

Charlie Hough possessed unusual longevity, as he pitched in the 1970s for the Dodgers and the 1980s for the Texas Rangers and spent two years apiece with the Chicago White Sox and Florida Marlins. He led the American League with 17 complete games in 1984 and 285 innings pitched in 1986. *Courtesy of the Los Angeles Dodgers.*

**24. Tom Candiotti, RP (1992–97), 52-64**. Candy played six years with the Dodgers and ended up winning 52 and losing 64. His best years were with Cleveland, with whom he won 73 games. He had eight years in which he won in double figures. His ERA with the Dodgers was 3.23—pretty respectable. Candy was born in Walnut Creek, California, in 1957 and played sixteen seasons in the majors, piling up 151 wins and 164 losses with a 3.73 ERA. He signed after playing college ball with St. Mary's College of California in Moraga.

**23. Derek Lowe, RP (2005–8), 54-48**. Lowe was big at six feet, six inches and had pretty good control, but he was more of a stuff pitcher. Born in 1973 in Michigan, he was drafted by Seattle and had some good years with Boston before settling with the Dodgers in 2005. He won 12, 14, 15 and 16 games, respectively, over four years, with an ERA of 3.59, before moving on to Atlanta, where he enjoyed three years with win totals of 15, 16 and 9, giving him a total of 166 wins over fifteen years through 2011. He was pitching for Cleveland in 2012.

**22. Ishmael Valdez, RP (1994–2000), 61-57**. Valdez came out of Mexico to the Dodgers at the age of twenty in 1994 and proceeded to win 61 games in six years with LA. He lost 57 over the same period, posted an ERA of 3.48 and didn't walk a lot of batters. He lasted 12 seasons, winning 104 games and losing 105 with an ERA of 4.09. Valdes was one of eighty major-league players linked with steroid use by the Mitchell report. His last year was 2005.

**21. Stan Williams, RP (1958–62), 57-46**. Stan was what you might call a "real Dodger." Born in New Hampshire, Stan was a strapping six-foot, four-inch 220-pounder who threw some serious heat. In 1961, he was second in strikeouts in the National League with 210. (Koufax was first and Drysdale was third as the

STAN WILLIAMS  P

Stan Williams was a tall power pitcher who notched all-star years with the Dodgers, Yankees and Twins and also pitched for the Indians, Cardinals and Red Sox. In fourteen years in the big leagues, Williams logged 109 wins and 94 losses. *TCMA.*

Dodgers captured all three top spots.) Stan won 109 games in fourteen seasons, five years winning in double figures. He even won a game for the Dodgers in the 1959 World Series. Stan averaged 6.8 strikeouts a game but 4.14 walks, which is a little high, but his Dodger ERA is 3.83. In 1970, with Minnesota, Stan went 10-1 in saves with an ERA of 1.99, one of the best ERA seasons that a relief pitcher has ever had. Stan was a pitching coach in the majors for fourteen years with Boston, the New York Yankees, Cincinnati, the Chicago White Sox and Seattle. Recently, he was an advance scout for the Washington Nationals.

**20. Andy Messersmith, RP (1973–75), 55-34.** Andy was a great pitcher for the Dodgers, winning 55 games, with a terrific ERA of 2.67. He was born in New Jersey and was drafted by the California Angels in 1966, winning 16 games in 1969 and 20 in 1971. He had three great years with Dodgers, winning 14, 20 and 19 games. He is best known for his part in ending the reserve clause. Andy held out in the 1975 season and ended up having one of his best years, with 19 wins and a National League–leading ERA of 2.19. He asked for a no-trade contract and ended up pitching without a contract at all. The *Sporting News* reported that Messersmith said, "It was less of an economic issue at the time than a fight for the right to have control over your own destiny…It was a matter of being tired of going in to negotiate a contract and hearing the owners say, 'OK, here's what you're getting. Tough luck.'" Messersmith went on to sign a three-year contract with Atlanta for $1 million, but he was thereafter plagued with injuries. Andy's lifetime ERA of 2.81 is the fourth highest in the majors since 1920. Not bad! He was a terrific pitcher who was dogged by injuries.

**19. Kevin Brown, RP (1999–2003), 58-32.** Kevin Brown should have been one of the Dodger greats. Well, that's pushing it a little, but he came to the Dodgers with great credentials. He won 150 games in twelve years. He arrived with the Dodgers in 1999 with a contract for seven years for $105 million—the first $100 million man in baseball. He promptly went 18-9. Then he went downhill, posting consecutive years of 13, 10, 3 and 14 wins. He seemed to have all the pitches—a fastball that averaged ninety-three to ninety-six miles per hour, a sharp slider and a split-fingered fastball. His biggest obstacle might have been his attitude. Brown was born James Kevin Brown in Milledgeville, Georgia, and played three years for Georgia Tech before signing with the Texas Rangers, for whom he led the AL with 21 wins in 1992. Brown ended up at 58-32 with the Dodgers, with a great ERA of 2.83 and a winning percentage of .664, making him third on the all-time Dodgers list. His last year was 2005, ending his career with a nice 211 victories, ninetieth all time.

**18. Chad Billingsley, RP (2006–2011), 70-56**. Billingsley has the stuff to be a great one but has not delivered yet. Chad has won 70 games for the Dodgers and lost 56. In six years, he has certainly been consistent, winning 7, 12, 16, 12, 12 and 11, respectively, with an ERA of 3.68. He has started 163 games and won 70. He registered 8 strikeouts per nine innings and 3.9 walks, which is quite a lot. Billingsley was a first-round pick of the Dodgers in 2003. He signed for $1.3 million. He pitched in the minor leagues until he was called up to the Dodgers in 2006. Billingsley signed a three-year, $35 million extension in spring 2011. Talk about having a good agent! He's still pitching for the Dodgers.

**17. Chan Ho Park, RP (1994–2001, 2008), 84-58**. Park, a six-foot, two-inch 210-pounder from Kongju, South Korea, won a mind-boggling 84 games for the Dodgers and lost only 58. Park came to the Dodgers in 1994 at age twenty-one and pitched eight straight years before returning again in 2008. In his top years, he won 18, 15, 14 and 14, respectively, for the Dodgers. He had a 3.77 ERA, and he struck out 8.3 batters per every nine innings he pitched. He pitched for seven teams over seventeen seasons, winning a total of 124 games. He retired after the 2010 season at age thirty-seven.

Leftie Doug Rau won 80 games with the Dodgers and only lost 58. He had five great years when he won 73 games, an average of 14.6 per year. His lifetime ERA was 3.30. *Courtesy of the Los Angeles Dodgers.*

**16. Doug Rau, LP (1972–79), 80-58**. A six-foot, two-inch left-hander from Texas, Rau won 80 games and lost 58 for the Dodgers. His ERA of 3.30 was outstanding. Doug had winning years of 13, 15, 16, 14 and 15. He pitched for Texas A&M and was a first-round pick by the Dodgers in 1970. Rau is best known for the row he had with Tommy Lasorda on the mound in Game 4 of the 1977 World Series, when he gave up four straight hits to the Yankees, and the Dodgers lost the game, 4-2. Rau only pitched nine years in the majors, eight with the Dodgers, winning a total of 81 games. He played a year for the Angels in 1981, winning 1, before hanging it up.

**15. Bill Singer, RP (1964–72), 69-76**. Singer pitched fourteen years in the bigs, nine seasons with the Dodgers, with whom he won 69 games with an ERA of 3.03. Singer, who was six feet, four inches and 184 pounds, hailed from Pomona, California. He was signed by the Dodgers in 1961 but did not make his major-league debut until September 1964, pitching six innings in his first game and allowing just one run. Bill pitched only a little for three years but became a full-fledged starter in 1967, when he won 12 games. He won 13 in 1968 and 20 in 1969. He pitched his no-hitter against the Phillies July 20, 1970, winning 5–0. He won 10 games in 1971, and he won only 6 and lost 16 in 1972. He was dealt to the Angels, turned himself around and won 20 games in 1973. He never did much after that, totaling a record of 69-76 with the Dodgers. He ended up winning 114 games in fourteen seasons with five clubs. After retiring, he has held various scouting positions with the Dodgers, Florida Marlins and Pittsburgh Pirates. He was fired as special assistant to the general manager for the New York Mets when he was accused of making racially insensitive remarks to Dodger executive Kim Ng. He later apologized and is still working in baseball. He is ranked this high, because I think he is better than the pitchers below him.

**14. Hideo Nomo, RP (1995–98, 2002–4), 81-66**. Hideo Nomo had a great rookie season and pitched a no-hitter with the Dodgers but, as a matter of course, walked way too many batters. He averaged 3.9 walks per game and had an ERA of 3.75. Nomo won 81 and lost 66 for the Dodgers for a winning percentage of .551. Nomo was born in Japan and signed with the Dodgers in 1995, becoming the first Japanese player to relocate to the United States. He won the Rookie of the Year Award in 1995, pitched two no-hitters and spent thirteen years in the bigs with eight different clubs. His Dodgers no-hitter was on September 17, 1996—a defeat of Colorado, 9–0. He threw a second no-hitter for the Boston Red Sox on April 4, 2001, against the Baltimore Orioles, 3–0. He spent an initial three-year stint with the Dodgers, winning 43 games, and then returned for another three years starting in 2002, winning another 36 games. He had 123 wins in the majors

Bill Singer spent most of his major-league career in Southern California, pitching for the California Angels for three years after his Dodger years. He also won 20 for the Angels, going 20-14 in first American League season, 1973. *Courtesy of the Los Angeles Dodgers.*

and 78 in Japan. He introduced Asian fans to Dodger stadium…and sushi soon followed as a concession item.

**13. Jerry Reuss, LP (1975–87), 86-69**. Jerry won 86 games for the Dodgers with 3.11 ERA and averaged only 2.1 walks per nine innings. Reuss was raised in St. Louis and came to the Dodgers after ten years with the Cards, Houston and Pittsburgh. He had years of 18, 10, 18, 12 and 14 wins for the Dodgers. He also had years where he won 14, 16, 16, 18, 14, 10 and 13 with other clubs. Jerry lost 70 games for the Dodgers but he ended up winning 220 games in the bigs—not chopped liver. He became a color commentator for the Dodgers in 2006. In 1980, Reuss had one of his best seasons with the Dodgers, going 18-6 with an 8–0 no-hitter against the San Francisco Giants on June 27. He finished second in the Cy Young Award balloting that year to Steve Carlton. In 1981, Reuss went 10-4 with an ERA of 2.30 in the strike-shortened season. He won 2 games in the playoffs and 1 against the New York Yankees, helping the Dodgers to win the World Series.

**12. Johnny Podres, LP (1958–66), 95-74**. Johnny Podres was dear to the hearts of the Dodgers longtime faithful for beating the Yankees in the final game of the 1955 World Series, 2–0. I stayed home on the farm from school and listened to the radio as Gil Hodges drove in both runs and Johnny put the Yankees in their rightful place. It marked the Brooklyn Dodgers' first and only championship, as well as the first time that they demolished the Yankees. Podres went on to a successful career in Los Angeles, winning 95 games in L.A. while losing 74 to post a winning percentage of .562. Podres, born near Lake Champlain in Witherbee, New York, the son of a coal miner, signed with Brooklyn in 1953. At the age of twenty-two, he beat the Yanks twice in the 1955 World Series, hurling complete games, and was named Most Valuable Player. His best year in L.A. was 1961, when he went 18-5 and had the best winning percentage in the National League. Podres went 4-1 overall in the fall classic, also helping the Dodgers win in 1959, 1963 and 1965. Podres ended up playing fifteen seasons, winning 148 games and losing 116. He had 24 shutouts and a lifetime ERA of 3.68. Johnny served as a pitching coach for thirteen seasons with San Diego, Boston, Minnesota and Philadelphia. Podres was married with two sons. He died of heart and kidney ailments in 2008. He is forever ensconced in Dodgers lore…and in my heart.

**11. Ramon Martinez**, **RP (1988–98), 123-77**. Ramon won 123 games for the Dodgers. In fact, his winning percentage was .615, which is sixth on the L.A. Dodgers' all-time list. Martinez, who was born in the Dominican Republic in 1968, made his major-league debut in 1991 at age twenty. His best year was in 1990, when he went 20-6 for the Dodgers with an ERA of 2.92. Ramon pitched eleven years for the Dodgers with winning seasons of 17, 10, 12, 17, 15 and 10. Among the team's bigger faux pas occurred in 1994: the Dodgers kept Ramon and let his brother, Pedro, escape to the Montreal Expos. Pedro, of course, went on to become one of the best pitchers in baseball, winning the Cy Young Award three times. Meanwhile, the Dodgers kept Ramon, whose overall ERA for the Dodgers was 3.44. Not bad. Ramon always said that Pedro was better than he was. That's one time the Dodgers should have listened. Ramon retired in 2001.

Burt Hooton, an unsmiling Texan whom Tommy Lasorda nicknamed "Happy," won 112 games for the Dodgers, including 18 in 1975 and 19 in 1979. His ERA for the ten years he spent with L.A. was 3.14. *Courtesy of the Los Angeles Dodgers.*

**10. Burt Hooton, RP (1975–84), 112-84**. Many in the top 10 did not win as many games as Ramon Martinez, but they some had other merits. Hooton went 112-84 for the Dodgers from 1975 through 1984. His ERA was an excellent 3.14. This Texan registered six years of double-digit wins. Burt, who was born in 1950, was a star for the University of Texas at Austin and was the second pick of the Chicago Cubs in the 1971 draft. Remarkably, he pitched a no-hitter in his fourth game. He went on to win 53 games in five years before going to the Dodgers in 1975, when he won 18 games. In the next six years, Burt won 11, 12, 19, 11, 14 and 11 respectively. He had

19 wins and an ERA of 2.28 and finished second in the Cy Young Award balloting in 1978. Burt also showed up big in the World Series. In 1977, he pitched a complete game victory in Game 2 against the Yankees, winning 6–1, retiring fourteen of the last fifteen hitters. He won Game 2 in 1978, beating the Yanks again, 4–3. In 1981, Hooton finished 11-6 in the strike-shortened season with a great ERA of 2.28. He beat the Houston Astros, 6–1, in Game 3 of the 1981 Division Series, allowing only three hits. Then he beat Montreal twice in NLCS, in Game 1, 5–1, and in Game 4, 7–1. He was named MVP of the series with an ERA of zero. In the World Series, he won Game 6, beating the Yankees, 9–2, to help the Dodgers become World Champions. Burt won 151 games in 15 years with an excellent ERA of 3.38. Nicknamed "Happy" for his unassuming nature, Hooton served as a pitching coach for the Houston Astros and the Oklahoma City Red Hawks, an Astros minor-league team.

**9. Bob Welch, RP (1978–87), 115-86.** Bobby Welch pitched from 1978 to 1987, won 115 and lost 86 for a .572 percentage. Born in Detroit, Michigan, Welch played college ball for Eastern Michigan. He joined the Dodgers at age twenty-one in 1978 and was renowned for a blazing fastball. He played eleven years for the Dodgers, posting seasons with 14, 16, 15, 13, 14 and 15 wins. He is known for striking out Reggie Jackson with two men on and two out in the top of the ninth inning in the 1978 World Series (at age twenty-one). He saved Game 5 of the 1981 NLDS against Montreal. As good as Welch was for the Bums, he pitched even better for the Oakland A's. He won the Cy Young Award for Oakland in 1990 when he won 27 games, following two years of 17 victories apiece. No pitcher has won that many games since. Welch ended up winning 211 games for the Dodgers and the A's. He was a great pitcher, averaging 6.4 strikeouts and 2.8 walks per nine innings for L.A. Welch wrote a book with George Vecsey of the *New York Times*, chronicling Welch's battle with alcoholism. He was pitching coach for the Arizona Diamondbacks when they won the World Series in 2001, and his son, Riley Welch, was a pitcher for the University of Hawaii baseball team.

**8. Tommy John, LP (1972–78), 87-42.** Not only was Tommy John a tough guy and a good pitcher, he also had that intangible extra dimension that invited fan response. Tommy won 87 games for the Dodgers, losing only 42, giving him a won-lost percentage of .674, the best of all the L.A. Dodgers. Tommy was born in Terre Haute, Indiana, and was signed by the Cleveland Indians in 1963 when he was twenty years old. He went to

BOB WELCH DODGERS

ROOKIE STRIKES OUT REGGIE JACKSON IN NINTH; DODGERS WIN GAME TWO IN WORLD SERIES 1978

Bob Welch struck out Reggie Jackson as a twenty-one-year-old rookie in the 1978 World Series with two men on base and two out in the top of the ninth inning of Game 2. This piece by artist Merv Corning commemorated that moment. *Courtesy of Tula Corning.*

the Chicago White Sox in 1965 and proceeded to win 82 games in seven years. But he moved on to the Dodgers, with whom he made a big name for himself. He had six straight years of double-digit wins for the Dodgers, winning 20 in 1977. He appeared in the All-Star Games in 1978, 1979 and 1980 and played in three World Series, all losses, two with the Dodgers and one with the Yankees. He had a great 2.97 ERA for the Dodgers, allowing 2.2 walks per nine innings.

In the 1977 National League Championship Series, Tommy beat Philadelphia, 4–1, a complete game victory that clinched the NL pennant for the Dodgers. In the scheme of the Dodgers-Yankees World Series rivalry, Tommy's stars were misaligned. He was on the losing side in 1977 and 1978 with the Dodgers versus the Yankees and in 1981 for the Yankees versus the World Champion Dodgers. In the 1977 World Series, John lost Game 3 to Mike Torrez and the Yanks, 5–3. In 1978, Tommy won the first game against the Yankees, 11–5. In Game 4, Tommy left in the eighth inning of a 3–3 deadlock. The Dodgers went on to lose, and that was it for John. In 1981, his team lost again, but John won Game 2 with a 3–0 shutout.

In 1974, when he was sailing along with a 13-3 record, John tore his ulnar collateral ligament in his left arm. Dr. Frank Jobe replaced the ligament with one from John's right forearm. John sat out the entire 1975 season, in which teammate Mike Marshall taught John a different way of pitching so as not to injure his knee or arm. John won 10 games in 1976 but miraculously came back and won 20 in 1977 and 17 in 1978. The innovative surgery became known in sports, especially baseball, as "Tommy John surgery." However, the brilliant Dodgers allowed him to escape to the dreaded Yankees, for whom he won 21 games in 1979 and 22 in 1980. Tommy went on to pitch seventeen years after the operation for a remarkable total of twenty-six years in the big leagues, winning 288 games and losing 231. Tommy has not been elected to the Hall of Fame, although his 288 wins certainly qualify him. He has been rejected so many times that it's up to the Veteran's Committee now, and if its members don't vote him in by 2024, he will be relegated to HOF Purgatory, as they say.

Tommy had four sons. When Travis John was two, he fell thirty-seven feet out of a window of their vacation home and landed on a car fender, but he later made a full recovery. His son Taylor, who appeared in *Les Misérables* on Broadway as a singer-actor, died at age twenty-eight in 2010 from an accidental overdose of prescription drugs. Tommy has persevered and is still active in baseball as a commentator and coach.

**7. Clayton Kershaw, LP (2008–2010), 47-28**. This is called wishful thinking, ranking Clayton Kershaw next. But he just may end up being one of the best pitchers of all time, barring anything unforeseen. Clayton, who comes out of Dallas, Texas, is six feet, three inches and 215 pounds—a left-hander who throws bullets. He started pitching for the Dodgers in 2008, winning 47 games and losing 28 through 2011. His ERA for that period was 2.87, and he averaged 9.3 strikeouts a game, but with 3.5 walks. He may be the Dodgers' best pitching prospect since Koufax. He has incrementally cut down his walks and increased strikeouts. He is said to have pitched a perfect game in a high school playoff, striking out every batter. Clayton was born on March 19, 1988, and only the sky is his limit. He posted four straight years of 5, 8, 13 and 21 victories. He won the pitching Triple Crown in 2011 with 21 wins, 248 strikeouts and an ERA of 2.48.

When Sandy Koufax was compared to him, Foxsports.com reported Sandy to say, "If he's as good as I think he is going to be, I'm honored."

Koufax said his influence on Clayton has been minimal: "I have not had a great deal to do with his success," Sandy said. "He had a good year but you can always get better…The ceiling is time, health. How long you want to play, how long you are able to play. You don't know…He's not satisfied. He wants to get better." The Dodgers are hoping.

**6. Claude Osteen, LP (1965–73), 147-126**. Claude Osteen is among the 1960s pitchers who instilled a sense of big-time winning in the Dodgers and made the Los Angeles Dodgers who they are. Born Claude Wilson Osteen in Casey Springs, Tennessee, Osteen was signed by the Cincinnati Reds in 1957, when he was seventeen years old. He pitched eight years for Cincy and the Washington Senators before being traded to the Los Angeles Dodgers for Pete Richert and Frank "Hondo" Howard. Osteen then found his groove, winning 15, 17, 17, 12, 20, 16, 14, 20 and 16 games, respectively, in those nine years. Osteen was 147-126 for the Dodgers, with an ERA of 3.09, walking only 2.1 batters per nine innings. Osteen twice won 20 games and was very efficient in the World Series.

In 1965, after Koufax and Drysdale had lost, Osteen pitched a shutout and had an ERA of 0.68 in that series—in which he pitched 21 innings of postseason play! In 1966, in the third game of the World Series against Baltimore, he allowed three hits and a run in 7 innings, but the Dodgers ended up losing the game and the series. In 1969, Osteen won 20 games, pitched 321 innings, had 183 strikeouts, 7 shutouts, 16 complete games and 41 starts. He pitched 3,460 innings in eighteen years for an average of 192 innings per year. That's quite a career for a five-foot, eleven-inch 160-pound southpaw. Osteen had a lifetime batting average of .188 with eight home runs and 76 RBIs. Claude ranks forty-fourth all-time in shutouts with 40 and seventy-first in total games pitched. He retired after the 1975 season. He became a pitching coach and plied that trade for St. Louis, Philadelphia, Texas and the Dodgers, as well as several minor-league teams. He is still missed on the Dodger Stadium mound.

**5. Fernando Valenzuela, LP (1980–90), 141-116**. Fernando ranks ahead of Claude because, with both at their best, Fernando was more overpowering and effective. Fernando, however, was also an icon, of the Dodgers, of baseball itself and of the tradition of great Latino players. Few athletes have ever made the kind of indelible impression that this burly Mexican made on the Los Angeles sporting scene when he arrived in the 1980s. The Dodgers bought his contract for $120,000 in 1979. He actually had already made his debut in 1980, winning 2 games. But he won 8 straight to start the 1981 season, with "Fernandomania" overtaking L.A.—and a sport wounded by a strike—by storm. It might be safe to say that no one created the hysteria that the twenty-year-old Fernando did with his Ruthian stature and great screwball.

He also went 3-1 in the 1981 postseason, leading the Dodgers all the way to win the World Series. With L.A., Fernando ended up winning an overall 141 games and losing 116 with a 3.31 ERA in eleven seasons. Fernando was born in Sonora, Mexico, in 1960 and joined the Dodgers in 1980 at the ripe age of nineteen. The 1981 season was cut short by a devastating strike by the players, but Fernando managed to go 13-7 with 180 strikeouts and an ERA of 2.48; he also won the Cy Young Award, the Rookie of the Year Award and the Silver Slugger Award. Fernando won his first 8 games, 4 of them by shutout, before he lost a game. In the World Series, the Dodgers beat the Yankees in 6 games, with Fernando getting the win in Game 3, 5–4.

Fernando also was quite a batsman. He hit .215 (pretty good for a pitcher) and struck out only nine times in sixty-four at bats in his rookie year to win the National League Silver Slugger Award. His best year at the plate was 1990, his last year with the Dodgers, when he hit .305, with 5 doubles, 1 home run and 11 RBIs. He won in double figures during nine of the eleven years he pitched. He also won 13 games for the San Diego Padres in 1996. Fernando was inducted into the Hispanic Heritage

Fernando Valenzuela had one of the greatest seasons a rookie ever had in 1981. He won his first 8 decisions, won the Cy Young Award and led the Dodgers to the World Series championship. *Courtesy of Upper Deck.*

Baseball Museum Hall of Fame in 2003. He was also named one of three starting pitchers for Major League Baseball's Latin Legends Team (along with Juan Marichal and Pedro Martinez). Valenzuela has been a Spanish-language color commentator with mainstay Jaime Jarrin and the Dodgers since 2003.

## 4. Orel Hershiser, RP (1983–94, 2000), 135-107.

Orel did not win as many games for the Dodgers (135) as Fernando did, but at the heights of both of their talents, Hershiser was the better pitcher. For Dodger fans, this is a lot like choosing one honored son over the other. Very few hurlers ever had a season to equal Hershiser's in 1988. He

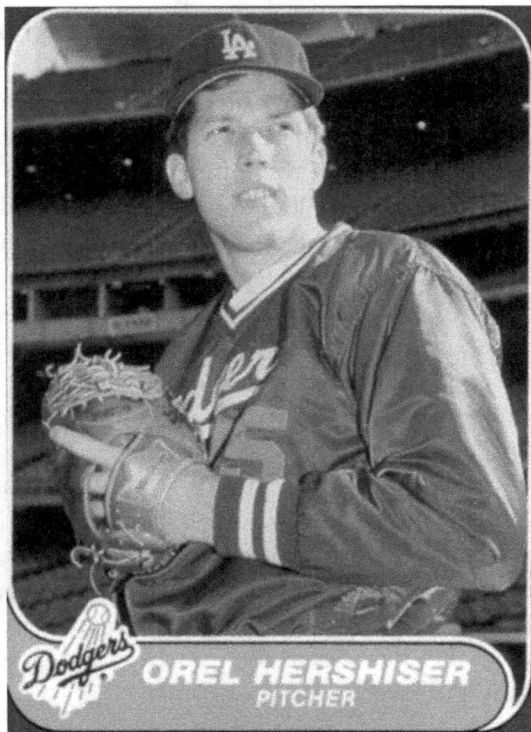

In 1985, Orel Hershiser was 19-3 with an ERA of 2.03 and finished third in the Cy Young Award voting to Dwight Gooden of the New York Mets. Hershiser went on to win 135 games for the Dodgers, with a lifetime ERA of 3.38. *Courtesy of Upper Deck.*

went 23-8, with an ERA of 2.26, 15 complete games and 8 shutouts. If that was not enough, he finished the season with 59 consecutive scoreless innings to break Don Drysdale's major-league record. That season's highlights are impressive enough, but Orel also was phenomenal in the playoffs and later. He saved Game 4 of the NCLS against Mets. Then he won Game 7 with a 6–0 shutout. If that wasn't enough, in the World Series, Hershiser beat Oakland in Game 2, 6–0. Then he went on to win the fifth game, 5–2, clinching the series. He is the only player in history to win the Cy Young Award, the Championship Series Most Valuable Player and the World Series MVP in the same year. He also went a stunning 19-3 in 1985 with an ERA of 2.01 and finished third in the balloting for the Cy Young Award. Orel was still great in 1989, winning fifteen games with an

ERA of 2.31, but he suffered from chronic Los Angeles Dodgers' pitchers disease: lack of offensive support.

Hershiser was born in Buffalo, New York, in 1958 and signed with the L.A. Dodgers in 1979 after attending Bowling Green University. He spent four years in the minors before being called up to the Dodgers in 1983. Starting in 1984, his seasonal win totals were 11, 19, 14, 16, 23 and 15. Nicknamed "the Bulldog" by Tommy Lasorda for his competiveness, Hershiser wasn't an overpowering thrower but more a discerning ace, well-schooled at the cat-and-mouse intelligence needed to know the batters in the National League. He tore his rotator cuff in 1990 and returned thirteen months later to finish 7-2 and help the Dodgers make it to second place. It was a sad day for Dodger fans when the brass let him escape to Cleveland in 1995.

Orel proceeded to win 16, 15, 14, 11 and 13 games in the next five years for the Indians, San Francisco and the New York Mets. He returned to L.A. in 2000 to close out his career as a Dodger. The six-foot, three-inch 190-pound Hershiser had a great sinker, a good curveball and average speed. But his tenacity and control made him one of the Dodgers' greatest assets. He has served as a pitching coach with Texas and as a baseball analyst on ESPN.

**3. Don Sutton, RP (1966–80, 1988), 233-181**. "Little D" came to the Dodgers in April 1966 for Sandy Koufax's last year with the Dodgers. Also on the staff were Don Drysdale, Claude Osteen, Phil Regan, Ron Perranowski and Bill Singer. But Sutton, as the fourth starter, won 12 games with an ERA of 2.99—at twenty-one years old. Sutton pitched in the shadow of Drysdale in 1967 and 1968, but he emerged as one of the team's top hurlers in 1969, winning 17 games. It was his third straight year of double-digit wins, and he went on to have eighteen straight years of double-digit victories. Drysdale had double-digit wins twelve times in a row and Koufax six in a row. Sutton notched 233 wins for the Dodgers and 181 losses, giving him a .550 winning percentage. He also had a 3.09 Dodgers ERA and averaged 6.4 strikeouts per nine innings and only 2.3 walks. His strength was his durability, control and pitching smarts. He won 324 games in all and was elected to the Baseball Hall of Fame in 1998. His other noteworthy achievements include 58 shutouts, 5 one-hitters and 3,574 strikeouts for seventh on the all-time list. He had twelve seasons of 15 or more wins. He had a few unlucky records. He pitched nine scoreless innings seven times in his career without a decision—but, of course, he did

Consistency was Don Sutton's hallmark trait. He pitched for twenty-three years in the big leagues, mostly for the Dodgers, but also for the Astros, Brewers, A's and Angels. He ended his career as one of the top-ten all-time leaders in shutouts (58), innings pitched (5,282.1) and losses (256) and was second to Cy Young in games started (756) until Nolan Ryan surpassed him. *Courtesy of the Los Angeles Dodgers.*

that mostly for the lackluster Dodgers. He holds the record for most at bats without a home run, 1,354.

In the 1974 NLCS, Sutton beat the Pittsburgh Pirates in the first game, 2–0, and in the fourth game, 12–1. In the World Series, he was the only Dodger pitcher to win a game, beating Oakland, 3–2, in the second game. He pitched a 7–1 victory over Philadelphia to win Game 2 of the 1977 NCLS. In the World Series against the Yankees, he won Game 2, 7–1. In 1978, Sutton lost Games 3 and 6 to the Yankees.

After leaving the Dodgers, he won 106 games with Houston, Milwaukee, Oakland and California. He returned to L.A. in 1988 to win 3 games and retire a Dodger. He pitched in 15 postseason games and was 6-4 with an ERA of 3.66. Born in Clio, Alabama, in a tar-paper shack, Sutton's father was eighteen and his mother fifteen. After his father moved to Florida to find construction work, Sutton played football, baseball and basketball in high school. He led his team to two state finals in baseball, winning his junior year and losing, 2-1, in his last year. He attended Gulf Community College in Panama City, Florida, but after one year opted to sign with the Dodgers. Sutton played for the Sioux Falls Packers in the minor leagues and joined the Dodgers in 1966, at which time he almost instantly became a starter. Sutton was diagnosed with cancer in 2002 but continued to develop his broadcasting career. He has broadcast for the Dodgers, Atlanta Braves and Washington Nationals. He is an avid golfer, and his son, Daron, is a broadcaster for the Arizona

Diamondbacks. You can still call him Little D, but that is with a mighty big D. He has the most wins in all Dodger history by far.

**2. Don Drysdale, RP (1958–69), 187-152**. Drysdale notched "only" 187 wins for the Dodgers—compared to Sutton's 233—but still earns the no. 2 spot here because he was the better pitcher. Drysdale, the most intimidating pitcher in Dodger history, is second in this overall ranking only to Sandy Koufax—no big mystery there. "Big D" won 25 games in 1962 and 23 in 1965. His ERA was 2.83 in 1962 and 2.77 in 1965. He won the Cy Young Award in 1962 as his 25 victories led the Major Leagues. Big D was aggressive and intimidating, and his 154 hit batsmen is a modern-day record. In 1968, he set a major-league record with 6 consecutive shutouts. He was 3-3 in World Series play, but he helped the Dodgers win in 1959, 1963 and 1965. He ended his career with 209 victories, 2,486 strikeouts, 167 complete games and 49 shutouts. Drysdale was also a very good hitter for a pitcher; he notched 218 hits with his bat, as well as 29 home runs.

Born in Van Nuys, California, Drysdale started out playing all the positions. It was not until his dad said that if he wanted to go further in baseball, he would have to do so as a pitcher. Don started taking pitching seriously. All of a sudden, he started growing while he pitched in high school. And in April 1954, he threw a no-hitter and struck out twelve batters against Hollywood High. Soon scouts were looking at him, and he decided to sign with the Dodgers. In 1955, he went to spring training in Vero Beach, Florida, and met the Dodgers. He was overcome at the respect with which players treated him—a kid. He vowed to remain a Dodger for life, and he was.

He had an 11-11 record with the Brooklyn Dodgers' Montreal farm team in 1955 and in April 1956 was called into Buzzie Bavasi's office and told he had made the big-league club. Drysdale made his debut on opening day in 1956. He won only 5 games that year, but 4 of them were against the hated New York Giants. His first major-league victory came April 24, 1956, against the Philadelphia Phillies, 6–1. Drysdale struck out nine batters and only walked one. He struck out the side in the first inning, and catcher Roy Campanella said he was the closest thing to the great side-arming Ewell Blackwell that he had ever seen. Drysdale was only nineteen and on a pennant-winning club. He pitched only 99 innings that year, but in 1957 he was the ace of the club, going 17-9, with an ERA of 2.69, 221 innings, 148 strikeouts and 61 walks.

The Dodgers' first year in California, 1958, was rough. Drysdale went 12-13 with a 4.17 ERA. He returned to 17 victories in 1959, helping the Dodgers to the World Series. He won Game 3 of the World Series, 3–1, as the Dodgers captured their first World Series victory in L.A. Drysdale was brilliant in 1962, but the injury to Koufax sidelined the team, and the Dodgers ended up blowing the special NL playoff series to the Giants—again, as in 1951, in three games. In the deciding third game, the Dodgers were leading 4–1 in the ninth inning when all hell broke loose. Matty Alou singled to lead off, followed by a force out of Matty at second from Harvey Keunn and walks to Willie McCovey and Felipe Alou to load the bases. A line-drive single by Willie Mays scored Keunn. Obviously, it was thought to bring in the ace of the staff, Drysdale, to put out the fire.

"[Leo] Durocher got real vocal in the dugout. He kept saying Drysdale should go in," Maury Wills said, as recounted in Steve Delsohn's *True Blue*. "Well, Walt [Manager Alston] didn't like it that it was coach Durocher's idea and not his. So he kind of cut off his nose to spite his face." In the same book, catcher Johnny Roseboro recalled, "Holy shit. It got ugly. Drysdale had volunteered to come in, and Alston wanted to save him for the World Series." After the game, Roseboro continued, "Alston went into his office and wouldn't come out. Guys were yelling, 'Come out, you gutless son of a bitch.'" Drysdale eventually helped win two World Series, but he had to wait until 1963 and 1965.

Drysdale pitched brilliantly in Game 3 of the 1963 World Series, beating the hated Yanks, 1–0, on a three-hitter. That helped the Bums to sweep the Yanks in four straight, allowing the Bombers only four runs and an amazingly anemic .171 batting average—the lowest in history at that time, from a team that boasted Mickey Mantle, Roger Maris, Yogi Berra, Joe Pepitone, Tony Kubek and Bobby Richardson.

In the 1965 World Series, things got curiouser and curiouser as Drysdale and Koufax blew the first two games to Minnesota, 8–2 and 5–1. However, Claude Osteen righted the ship with a 4–0 shutout at Dodger Stadium, and this was followed by Drysdale beating the Twins in Game 4, 7–2, leaving it up to buddy Koufax to shut them out in Games 5 and 7 to win the World Championship. Drysdale had double-digit wins every year until his last year in 1969, when he retired after pitching only 62 innings.

Drysdale entered his broadcasting career and worked for the Montreal Expos, Chicago White Sox, California Angels and Texas Rangers before settling in with the Dodgers. Drysdale announced Steve Garvey's home run that helped the Padres win their only National League pennant. He also announced Kirk Gibson's memorable home run when, in Game 1 of the 1988 World Series, he came off the bench, gimpy, and hit the game-winning shot. Drysdale was married twice, the second time to former basketball player Ann Meyers, with whom he had three children. Drysdale died of an apparent heart attack in his hotel room in July 1993, during a broadcast stint of Dodger games. His autobiography *Once a Bum, Always a Dodger* was published in 1990. I still misses him.

**1. Sandy Koufax, LP (1958–66), 156-77.** If I could start a team today and had a choice of any baseball pitcher in history, I would select Sandy Koufax. (The only other possible considerations would be, in order, Christy Mathewson, Walter Johnson, Warren Spahn and Bob Gibson.) There was nothing to dislike about Koufax. There's testimony enough to him being the best pitcher or best southpaw anyone has ever witnessed. He performed his best whenever the team had to count on him. His self-effacing, unassuming personality appealed to the fans. He was the perfect physical specimen of height (six feet, two inches) and weight (210 pounds). He developed inner strength and strength of character simultaneously with his athletic skills, and as a mid-career interviewee and post-baseball personality, his natural laugh and smile were contagious. He was born in Brooklyn of Jewish descent, a star basketball player and a pitcher. When he came to the Dodgers, he was nineteen years old.

Fans of Brooklyn watched Koufax's growth as a pitcher with fascination. Manager Walt Alston had second thoughts about using him because he threw so wildly. He would take him out even when Koufax was pitching solidly because the manager was afraid that the pitcher might veer into a stretch of wild pitches and blow the game for the Dodgers. Veteran catcher Rube Walker remembered Koufax as being "nervous fast."

"Sometimes he had real problems early and just couldn't get with it," Brooklyn Dodgers staff pitcher Carl Erskine said. "But if he got into a groove early, he was awesome. He was just not polished enough or refined enough to be consistent. Sandy's struggles were with himself to bring himself to a major-league level as a pitcher...On any given day he was awesome. But then two outings after that, he'd have trouble getting out of the first inning. But the potential was definitely there."

In his first three years in Brooklyn, Koufax pitched in 62 games and posted a record of 9-10. He struck out only three more than he walked. The fans waited for him to explode into stardom. When he had a good game, this particular Dodgers fan was beside himself. On June 4, 1957, Sandy struck out

Sandy Koufax was the most dominant National League pitcher of the 1960s. In the voting for the NL's Most Valuable Player, Koufax received some votes every year from 1961 through 1966, the year of his sudden retirement. In 1963, he won the MVP with 237 votes (to no. 2 Dick Groat's 190). In 1965, Willie Mays won with 224 (to No. 2 Sandy with 177). In 1966, Roberto Clemente won the MVP, just edging out Sandy, 218 votes to 208. *Drawing by Pat Lechman.*

6 of the first eight batters he faced. He eventually struck out 12 in seven-plus innings and finished the year with a 5-4 record, striking out 122 hitters in 104 innings. Koufax has the distinction of throwing the final pitch for Brooklyn when he struck out Willie Jones of the Phillies in the bottom of the eighth inning in 1957.

When the Dodgers moved to Los Angeles in 1958, Koufax showed little improvement, going 11-11. In 1959, he was 8-6 with a 4.06 ERA. Privately, Koufax thought the Dodgers were ready to give up on him. But Walt Alston had no such thoughts. "You can't give up on him," Alston said, in a brilliant understatement. On August 31, 1959, against the Giants, Sandy struck out eighteen batters to set a major-league record. Then, in the 1959 World Series, Koufax pitched two perfect innings of relief in the opener. He started Game 5 before 92,706 people in the Los Angeles Memorial Coliseum and pitched six innings in a losing effort, 1–0. Koufax pitched in two games of the series, posting seven strikeouts, five walks and an ERA of 1.00. It was only the start of things to come.

In 1960, however, Koufax finished 8-13 with an ERA of 3.91. He was so discouraged that he asked General Manager Buzzie Bavasi to trade him so that he could get a fresh start. Bavasi asked him how any team would pitch him when he couldn't get anyone out. Koufax told Erskine he was considering retiring. But Koufax's career started to turn around with input from three sources.

Pitching coach Joe Becker worked with his mechanics to help him both control and hide his pitches. Statistician Allan Roth pointed out how he was less effective against left-handed batters than right-handers when the opposite is usually true. So, Koufax altered the grip on his curve, making it drop down and away to lefties. Finally, catcher Norm Sherry convinced him not to overthrow, not to try to strike everyone out, to relax and throw strikes. Voila! Koufax was throwing harder than ever, but with better control.

As a result, Koufax started the 1961 season by beating the Cincinnati Reds, 5–2, to win in April for the first time in his career. Koufax, pitching regularly in the Dodgers rotation for the first time, won 6 straight games from mid-May to mid-June. Sixty-four games into the season, Koufax was 10-3. He shut out the Cubs on two hits, striking out 14. In trying to win 20 games, Koufax was throttled by St. Louis and then lost a 2–1 decision to the Phillies, allowing two unearned runs. But he struck out 7 Phils to reach 269 for the season, breaking the National league record of 267 set by Christy Mathewson in 1903. Sandy finished 18-13 on the year with an ERA of 3.91. More importantly, he had pitched 255 innings, struck out 269 and walked 96. It was the start of something big.

The year 1962 should have been an incredible one, but Koufax finished 14-7, saddled with a mysterious finger ailment. On April 24, however, he beat the Cubs, 10–2, and tied Bob Feller's major-league record of eighteen strikeouts in a game. On June 30, 1962, he threw his first no-hitter, beating the New York Mets, 5–0, striking out thirteen. The numbness of his finger had started in mid-May, so no one knew how he could even pitch—much less at the caliber he did. As his finger worsened, his pitching improved. He beat Warren Spahn and the Milwaukee Braves, 2–1, then Bob Gibson and St. Louis, 1–0.

When his uncle visited him, he told Sandy that his finger looked like a grape and that he thought he was crazy to try to pitch. At first, it was thought that Koufax had a blood ailment. But the truth was that he injured the digit when he was batting. A ball hit his hand and pinched a nerve that caused an infection around the cuticle. Gangrene was a big concern. Koufax called the pain intolerable, and it was even thought that his finger might have to be amputated. He left the Dodger lineup on July 17 when the Dodgers owned an eight-game NL lead, which they blew. Koufax tried pitching again at the end of the season, but he just wasn't effective. And the Dodgers ended up losing to the San Francisco Giants in a playoff—shades of 1951.

Koufax went into the next season hoping that his finger would be okay. It was. He had a sore shoulder, but that did not stop him. On May 11,

Koufax woke up the Dodgers, pitching his second no-hitter in two years, 8–0. Koufax pitched great, carrying a 14-3 record into the All-Star Game break. In a late-season game against the Cards, with the pennant on the line, Koufax won 4–0. From the sixth through the ninth inning, Koufax threw one pitch that was not a strike. Koufax ended the season with his best year, 25-5. He struck out 306 batters in 311 innings and notched 11 shutouts, a record for southpaws. His ERA was 1.88. Everyone was on Koufax's bandwagon, recognizing him as not only the best pitcher in baseball but also one of the best ever.

The Dodgers went into the World Series as underdogs against the mighty Yankees, but thanks to Koufax, the L.A. club swept the fall classic. Koufax won the first game, 5–2, and the fourth game, 2–1. He was named Most Valuable Player of the World Series, MVP of the National League, the Cy Young Award winner of baseball and Player of the Year as well as Pitcher of the Year by the *Sporting News*. It was one of the most incredible years in baseball history. And Sandy was not done.

Koufax opened the 1964 season with a 4–0 shutout of the St. Louis Cardinals. But he missed time early in the season with adhesions in his pitching arm. By the end of May, he was only 4-4. After a few bad starts, he faced the Philadelphia Phillies on June 4 and pitched his third no-hitter in as many years, 4–0. Koufax won ten of his next eleven games, but the Dodgers still trailed. Then, in August, Koufax injured his shoulder diving back into second on a pickoff attempt. His left elbow was swollen, but he made his next start, shutting out the Reds for 7 innings. He started four days later against the Cardinals, struck out thirteen and had his 15$^{th}$ win in his last sixteen starts. But when he woke up the next morning, his arm was swollen from wrist to shoulder. Diagnosed with traumatic arthritis, Koufax tried to pitch, but it was useless. He was done for the season. Sandy finished the year with an incredible 19-5 record with a 1.74 ERA and 223 strikeouts in 223 innings.

The 1965 season brought more agonizing news for Koufax. On March 31, after pitching a spring training game, Sandy woke up to find his arm hemorrhaging. Dr. Robert Kerlan told him that he would be lucky to pitch once a week. The team was in shock because of the terrible condition of Koufax's arm. Cortisone reduced the swelling, but Kerlan didn't like the idea of injecting him with shots twice a week and him worsening the condition by pitching. Finally, Koufax decided not to pitch between starts. He took drugs and iced his arm in a tub of near-freezing water. The start of his season was delayed a week, but on a rainy Sunday in Philadelphia, he beat the Phillies,

6–2. His elbow was sore and puffy, but Koufax was sure he could pitch. By the end of April, he was 4-2. Koufax, pitching through the pain and medication, did not miss a start the entire season. He won his 20th game on August 10. But as late as September 16, the Dodgers were four and a half games behind the Giants. The final game of a four-game series in San Francisco was played on August 22, 1965.

I witnessed the events as Koufax pitched for the Dodgers and the great Juan Marichal for the Giants. This is the game in which Marichal, batting, thought that catcher John Roseboro had thrown the ball back to Koufax too close to his ear, so the Giants hurler turned in the batter's box and clobbered Roseboro over the head with his bat. There was blood everywhere. The old lady sitting in front of me and my army buddies stood up and screamed, "Hit 'im again. Hit 'im again." I couldn't believe it. Koufax rushed to Roseboro's aid, and Willie Mays came off the on-deck circle to help wrestle Roseboro back from fighting Marichal. After things settled down, Koufax got a couple of outs, walked two and gave up a home run to Mays. The Giants won, 4–3, frustrating Koufax and the Dodgers.

Then Koufax suffered a five-game losing streak, but he ended it in style on September 8. He pitched a perfect game to beat the Cubs, 1–0. And he was the key to the Dodgers' winning of the pennant. On September 18, he shut out St. Louis, 1–0. On September 25, he shut out St. Louis again, 4–0. On September 29, he shut out the Cincinnati Reds, 5–0, and on October 3, he pitched with two days' rest and beat the Milwaukee Braves, 3–1, to win the pennant. That was not all. In the World Series, Sandy beat Minnesota in the fifth game, 7–0, and in the seventh game, 2-0, to clinch the World Championship.

"I think that final game was probably one of the greatest pitching performances I've ever seen," Minnesota slugger Harmon Killebrew said three decades later in Gruver's book. "Sandy pitched on two days' rest and shut us out two to nothing. I'll never forget that."

Once again, Koufax was MVP of the series and the Cy Young Award winner. Sandy finished 26-8 with a 2.04 ERA, pitching an incredible 335 innings with an astronomical 382 strikeouts and 71 walks…with an arm he could barely lift. Was he the man or what?

"Koufax is great," Twins manager Sam Mele said. "The best I believe I have ever seen."

Sandy's arm was so bad going into the 1966 season that teammates wondered if he could lift it, let alone pitch. And Koufax, who had made $85,000 in 1965, was looking to become the sport's highest-paid pitcher.

So he and teammate Don Drysdale formed an alliance to ask for three-year contracts totaling $1 million, which translated to $166,000 per year. They held out into spring training as long as they could, eventually settling for $125,000 for Koufax and $110,000 for Drysdale. Since most players are overpaid, they are two of the few guys in history who actually earned their salaries. Unfortunately, Don's career was going downhill, as he only finished 13-16 in 1966 in spite of the fact that the Dodgers won the pennant. Koufax, however, only got better. He had 16 wins by July 14 but was losing the feeling in the fingers of his left hand. His use of painkillers and ice baths increased. The opposition couldn't believe that he could be in such pain and still dominate.

"I am not gonna sit up all night and cry for him," Mets third baseman Kenny Boyer said. "He threw one pitch that was impossible. No ball can get up to the plate that quick. Then he threw it again."

Koufax never complained. Even Bavasi, who had arthritis himself in later years, said, "I don't see how he did it. Every pitch he threw, he must have had tears in his eyes."

The epitome of his 1966 year was the final game of the season against Philadelphia at Dodger Stadium. L.A. needed a win to clinch the pennant. Koufax's arm was in terrible shape, yet he went out and pitched his team to a victory, 6–3 for his 27th win. Koufax, with an arm about to fall off, led the league in games started with 41 and innings pitched with 323. And his ERA, a minuscule 1.73, was his best ever. But the Dodgers' lack of hitting caught up to them, and they went down in the series, four games to none, to the Baltimore Orioles. Koufax finished his most dominating season and won his third Cy Young Award.

On November 18, 1966, Koufax faced the media and said, "A few minutes ago, I sent a letter to the Dodgers asking to put me on the voluntarily disabled list. I feel I am doing the right thing. I've got a lot of years to live after baseball, and I would like to live them with the complete use of my body. I have taken too many pills and too many shots. I am just afraid that something might happen that would cost me the use of my arm the rest of my life." He was thirty years old, in the prime of his athletic years.

The greatest pitcher the game had ever known quit after his greatest season. He might have been the toughest guy, both mentally and physically, to ever play the game.

The 50 Greatest Los Angeles Dodgers Starters

| Rank | Years Played | Name | Total Games per 9 Innings | Total Innings | W-L | ERA (ER) | SO per 9 Innings (Total SO) | BB per 9 Innings (Total Innings) | W-L % |
|---|---|---|---|---|---|---|---|---|---|
| 1. | 1958-66 | Sandy Koufax | 235 | 2,119+ | 156-77 | 2.64 (622) | 9.4 (2,214) | 3.0 (709) | .670 |
| 2. | 1958-69 | Don Drysdale | 346 | 3,112 | 187-152 | 2.98 (1,029) | 6.6 (2,283) | 2.2 (763) | .552 |
| 3. | 1966-80, 1988 | Don Sutton | 424 | 3,816+ | 233-181 | 3.09 (1,311) | 6.4 (2,696) | 2.3 (996) | .563 |
| 4. | 1983-94, 2000 | Orel Hershiser | 242 | 2,180+ | 135-107 | 3.12 (755) | 6.0 (1,456) | 2.8 (667) | .558 |
| 5. | 1980-90 | Fernando Valenzuela | 261 | 2,348+ | 141-116 | 2.93 (764) | 6.7 (1,759) | 3.5 (915) | .549 |
| 6. | 1965-73 | Claude Osteen | 266 | 2397+ | 147-126 | 3.09 (822) | 4.4 (1,162) | 2.1 (568) | .538 |
| 7. | 2008-2011 | Clayton Kershaw | 80 | 716+ | 47-28 | 2.87 (229) | 9.3 (745) | 3.5 (278) | 6.27 |
| 8. | 1972-78 | Tommy John | 133 | 1,198 | 87-42 | 2.97 (396) | 4.9 (649) | 2.2 (296) | .674 |

| | Years | Name | | | W-L | ERA | | | |
|---|---|---|---|---|---|---|---|---|---|
| 9. | 1978–87 | Bob Welch | 202 | 1,820+ | 115-86 | 3.14 (635) | 6.4 (1,292) | 2.8 (556) | .572 |
| 10. | 1975–84 | Burt Hooton | 207 | 1,861+ | 112-84 | 3.14 (649) | 5.0 (1,042) | 2.6 (540) | .571 |
| 11. | 1988–98 | Ramon Martinez | 192 | 1,731+ | 123-77 | 3.45 (663) | 6.8 (1,314) | 3.7 (704) | .615 |
| 12. | 1958–66 | Johnny Podres | 156 | 1,407+ | 95-74 | 3.66 (572) | 6.1 (947) | 2.9 (458) | .562 |
| 13 | 1975–87 | Jerry Reuss | 156 | 1,407+ | 86-69 | 3.11 (486) | 4.4 (685) | 2.1 (333) | .555 |
| 14. | 1995–98, 2002–2004 | Hideo Nomo | 135 | 1,217+ | 81-66 | 3.74 (506) | 8.9 (1,200) | 3.9 (528) | .551 |
| 15. | 1964–72 | Bill Singer | 142 | 1,274+ | 69-76 | 3.03 (429) | 7.0 (989) | 2.8 (392) | .476 |
| 16. | 1972–79 | Doug Rau | 139 | 1,250+ | 80-58 | 3.30 (459) | 5.0 (694) | 2.7 (378) | .580 |
| 17. | 1994–2001, 2008 | Chan Ho Park | 142 | 1,279 | 84-58 | 3.77 (536) | 8.3 (1,177) | 4.2 (596) | .592 |
| 18. | 2006–2011 | Chad Billingsley | 113 | 1,013+ | 70-52 | 3.68 (414) | 8.0 (903) | 3.9 (441) | .574 |
| 19. | 1999–2003 | Kevin Brown | 97 | 872+ | 58-32 | 2.83 (274) | 8.1 (784) | 2.3 (223) | .644 |
| 20. | 1973–75 | Andy Messersmith | 103 | 926 | 55-34 | 2.67 (275) | 6.2 (637) | 2.9 (301) | .618 |

| Rank | Years Played | Name | Total Games per 9 Innings | Total Innings | W-L | ERA (ER) | SO per 9 Innings (Total SO) | BB per 9 Innings (Total Innings) | W-L % |
|------|--------------|------|---------------------------|---------------|-----|----------|------------------------------|----------------------------------|-------|
| 21. | 1958–62 | Stan Williams | 97 | 872 | 57-46 | 3.83 (371) | 6.8 (657) | 4.4 (429) | .553 |
| 22. | 1994–2000 | Ismael Valdez | 118 | 1,065 | 61-57 | 3.48 (412) | 6.6 (785) | 2.5 (299) | .517 |
| 23. | 2005–8 | Derek Lowe | 94 | 850+ | 54-48 | 3.59 (339) | 6 (563) | 2.3 (214) | .529 |
| 24. | 1992–97 | Tom Candiotti | 116 | 1,048 | 52-64 | 3.23 (416) | 6.2 (718) | 2.8 (329) | .448 |
| 25. | 1987–91 | Tim Belcher | 89 | 806 | 50-38 | 2.99 (268) | 7.0 (633) | 2.9 (261) | .568 |
| 26. | 1970–80 | Charlie Hough | 89 | 799+ | 47-46 | 3.50 (311) | 6.0 (536) | 5.7 (511) | .516 |
| 27. | 1971–77 | Al  Downing | 100 | 897+ | 46-37 | 3.16 (315) | 5.3 (532) | 3.3 (326) | .554 |
| 28. | 1974–78 | Rick Rhoden | 74 | 670+ | 42-24 | 3.40 (253) | 4.4 (325) | 2.7 (203) | .636 |
| 29. | 1992–97 | Pedro Astasio | 98 | 886+ | 48-47 | 3.68 (363) | 6.1 (598) | 2.8 (278) | .505 |

| # | Years | Name | | | | | | | | |
|---|---|---|---|---|---|---|---|---|---|---|
| 30. | 1994–2004 | Darren Dreiffort | 97 | 872+ | | 48-60 | 4.37 (423) | 8.3 (802) | 4 (389) | .444 |
| 31. | 2002–6 | Odalis Perez | 86 | 772+ | | 45-40 | 3.94 (338) | 6.2 (531) | 2 (169) | .529 |
| 32. | 2008–2011 | Hiroki Kuroda | 78 | 699 | | 41-46 | 3.45 (268) | 6.7 (523) | 2.1 (163) | .471 |
| 33. | 1991–94 | Kevin Gross | 76 | 680 | | 40-44 | 3.63 (274) | 6.9 (527) | 3.2 (244) | .476 |
| 34. | 2004–5 2009–2010 | Jeff Weaver | 63 | 567+ | | 38-29 | 4.21 (265) | 6.3 (400) | 2.6 (163) | .567 |
| 35. | 1983–87 | Rick Honeycutt | 72 | 651 | | 33-45 | 3.58 (259) | 4.9 (352) | 2.8 (186) | .423 |
| 36. | 2002–4 | Kazuhisa Ishii | 53 | 473 | | 36-25 | 4.30 (226) | 7.2 (382) | 5.8 (305) | .590 |
| 37. | 1989–91 | Mike Morgan | 67 | 600 | | 33-36 | 3.06 (204) | 4.7 (318) | 2.3 (154) | .478 |
| 38. | 1981–89 | Alejandro Pena | 85 | 769+ | | 3838 | 2.92 (250) | 6.7 (571) | 2.9 (244) | .500 |
| 39. | 1963–67 | Bob Miller | 66 | 597+ | | 29-33 | 3.03 (201) | 5.8 (386) | 3.2 (210) | .468 |
| 40. | 1958–61 | Roger Craig | 46 | 413 | | 26-15 | 3.70 (170) | 4.7 (214) | 3.3 (152) | .634 |
| 41. | 1987–89 | Tim Leary | 50 | 453+ | | 26-29 | 3.47 (175) | 6 (300) | 2.6 (128) | .473 |

| Rank | Years Played | Name | Total Games per 9 Innings | Total Innings | W-L | ERA (ER) | SO per 9 Innings (Total SO) | BB per 9 Innings (Total Innings) | W-L % |
|---|---|---|---|---|---|---|---|---|---|
| 42. | 1962–71 | Joe Moeller | 65 | 583+ | 26-36 | 4.01 (260) | 4.7 (307) | 2.7 (176) | .419 |
| 43. | 1969–72 | Pete Mikkelson | 31 | 275+ | 24-17 | 3.27 (100) | 6.1 (191) | 2.9 (90) | .585 |
| 44. | 1976–81 | Rick Sutcliffe | 45 | 405+ | 22-21 | 4.04 (182) | 4.3 (195) | 3.9 (174) | .512 |
| 45. | 1995–2000 | Antonio Osuna | 36 | 327 | 24-21 | 3.28 (119) | 9.6 (346) | 3.9 (141) | .533 |
| 46. | 2007 and 2009 | Randy Wolf | 35 | 317 | 20-13 | 3.72 (131) | 7.2 (254) | 2.8 (97) | .606 |
| 47. | 1999–2001 | Matt Herges | 26 | 234+ | 20-13 | 3.38 (88) | 6.5 (169) | 3.6 (94) | .606 |
| 48. | 2010–11 | Ted Lilly | 30 | 269+ | 19-18 | 3.85 (115) | 7.8 (235) | 2.2 (66) | .514 |
| 49. | 2002–4 and 2009 | Guillermo Mota | 33 | 294 | 18-14 | 2.79 (91) | 7.2 (239) | 3.2 (104) | .563 |
| 50. | 1991–92 | Bob Ojeda | 39 | 355+ | 18-18 | 3.40 (134) | 5.4 (214) | 3.9 (151) | .500 |

# Ranking of Los Angeles Dodger Relief Pitchers

Relief pitchers are a different breed of ballplayer. Years ago, they were the firemen who came in to put out the final embers. Then pitchers started to be called starters, middle relievers or closers. No one pitched nine innings anymore. A win in the Major Leagues since the 1980s is usually a collaborative effort. Many fans don't like it. I always enjoyed watching a pitcher from my team or the opponent's pitch a complete game. He weathered storms and came out on top—or even lost. But he persevered. Now, at the first sign of distress or just after five innings are logged, no matter what, a pitcher is yanked for a bullpen thrower, then another, then another and another. So goes strategy. That's what we live with. There's some apples-and-oranges aspects of selecting the best relief pitchers over L.A. Dodger history, because the game has changed so much.

**25. Yhency Brazoban (2004–8), 10-12, 21 saves**. Brazoban was from the Dominican Republic and pitched five years for the Dodgers. His ERA was kind of high at 4.70, and he only pitched 115 innings. Yhency started as an outfielder, but the Yankees converted him to a pitcher in 2003. He was acquired from the Yankees along with Jeff Weaver and Brandon Weedon in exchange for Kevin Brown in 2003. His big year for the Dodgers was 2005 when he set rookie records by appearing in 75 games and saving 21 as a replacement for the injured Eric Gagne. However, several injuries sidelined Brazoban, and he was released in 2009.

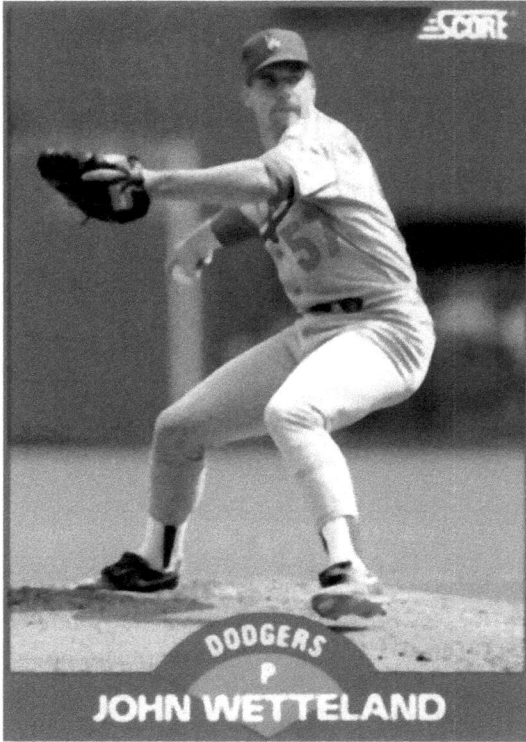

John Wetteland started his major-league career in L.A. in 1989 and became one of the most effective relief pitchers of his time, leading the American League with 43 saves in 1996 for the New York Yankees. *Courtesy of Panini America, Inc.*

**24. John Wetteland, RP (1989–91), 8-12, 1 save.** Wetteland was chosen for this spot because of what might have been. He pitched twelve years in the bigs and had a whopping 335 saves. The Dodgers drafted him in 1985 out of Santa Rosa, California, when he was eighteen years old. He made his debut with L.A. in 1989 at the age of twenty-two, going 8-12 and saving 1. He was traded to Cincinnati and then to Montreal and immediately became a premier relief pitcher, saving 37 games for the Expos. In 1996, he had 43 saves to lead the American League for the New York Yankees. Wetteland was named the World Series MVP for the Yankees that year in their defeat of the Atlanta Braves; he became the first pitcher to record 4 saves in a World Series. The Dodgers let Wetteland escape without uncovering his natural ability. Wetteland is married with four children and lives in Texas. He has served as a pitching coach for various teams and as an assistant college coach.

**23. Kuo, Hong Chi, LP (2005–2011), 13-17, 13 saves.** Born in Taiwan, Kuo came to the United States in 1999 when the Dodgers signed him for $1.25 million. Kuo underwent two "Tommy John surgeries" and was not able to pitch again until 2005. From 2005 to 2011, he was 13-17, with 13 saves and an ERA of 3.73. His best year was 2010, when he had 12 saves. He signed with the Seattle Mariners for 2012 season but was released.

**22. Scott Radinsky**, **LP (1996–98), 16-8, 17 saves**. Radinsky pitched for the Dodgers from 1996 to 1998 going, 16-8 with 17 saves and an ERA of 2.67 in that time. Scott was originally drafted in 1986 by the Chicago White Sox out of Simi High School in California. He pitched from 1990 to 1995 for the White Sox before coming to the Dodgers. He ended up with a lifetime record of 42-25 with 52 saves. His last season was 2001 with the Cleveland Indians, for whom he was pitching coach in 2012.

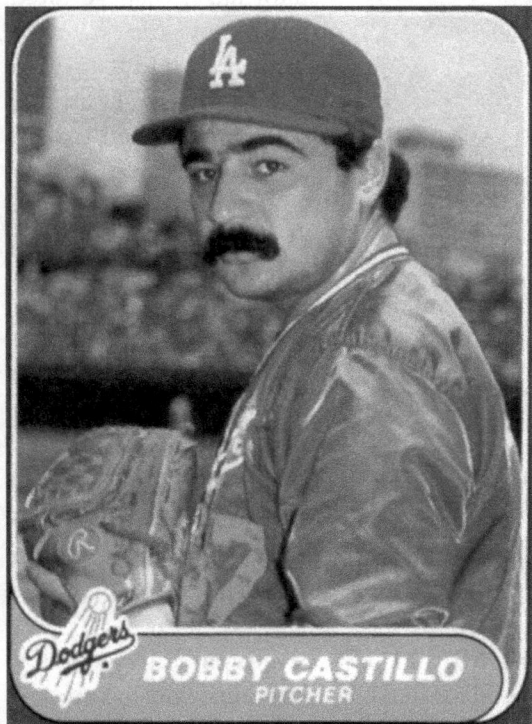

Bobby Castillo pitched six years for the Dodgers and was at his best in 1980 when he went 8-6 with a 2.75 ERA and 5 saves. He also threw three years for the Minnesota Twins, winning 23 games. *Courtesy of Upper Deck.*

**21. Bobby Castillo, RP (1977–81, 1985), 15-16, 18 saves**. Castillo pitched 286+ innings for the Dodgers, going 15-16 with an ERA of 3.90 and 18 saves. Drafted by Kansas City out of high school in Los Angeles, Castillo made his debut with the Dodgers in 1977 at age twenty-two. He pitched six years for the Dodgers, with his best year being 1980, when he finished 8-6 with a 2.75 ERA. Castillo pitched 689 innings in the Major Leagues, including three years with the Minnesota Twins.

**20. Roger McDowell, RP (1991–94), 17-19, 23 saves**. McDowell pitched 235+ innings for the Dodgers, with 23 saves, a record of 17-19 and an ERA of 3.48. McDowell, born in Cincinnati in 1960, was drafted by the New York Mets in 1982. He started pitching with the Mets in 1985 and came to the Dodgers in 1992. Always a prankster, he kept things on the lighter side. He made an important contribution to the Dodgers over a short period. He was pitching coach for the Atlanta Braves in 2012.

Terry Forster, from Sioux Falls, South Dakota, won 11 games and saved 27 for the Dodgers. But he lasted sixteen years in the big leagues, winning 54 games and saving 127 with a lifetime ERA of 3.23. *Courtesy of the Los Angeles Dodgers.*

**19. Terry Forster, RP (1978–82), 11-13, 27 saves**. Forster, who accrued 27 saves, pitched 207 innings with an ERA of 3.48 for the Dodgers. Forster, a native of Santee, California, was drafted in 1970 by the Chicago White Sox. He came to the bigs in 1971 at age nineteen and lasted sixteen years to collect 54 wins and an overall ERA of 3.48. He also pitched for the Pittsburgh Pirates, Atlanta Braves and California Angels, recording a total of 127 saves. He pitched 6 innings in the 1978 and 1981 World Series for the Dodgers, allowing no runs. He obviously contributed to a lot of clubs even without great stats.

**18. Clem Labine, RP (1958–60), 11-17, 24 saves**. Labine was a first-rate relief pitcher of his era. He had 24 saves and his won-lost record was 11-17 in his three years for the L.A. Dodgers after he led the NL in saves in 1956 with 19 and 1957 with 17 for Brooklyn. He pitched 205+ innings with an ERA of 4.21 in L.A. But he had some really big games. Labine was born in Lincoln, Rhode Island, but grew up in Woonsocket, the son of a weaver. After serving in World War II as a paratrooper, he was signed by the Dodgers in 1944. After mastering a sinkerball, he joined the Dodgers in 1950. He led the National League in saves in both 1956 (19) and 1957 (17). When he retired after the 1962 season, he was fourth in career saves with 96.

"If you had a lead, there was this thing where about the seventh or eighth inning, where he'd get up, sort of a ritual, and walk down to the bullpen,"

Roger Craig said in Bob Cairns's *Pen Men*, an oral history of relief pitching. "Clem was kind of a cocky, arrogant type, which was good. I liked it. He'd fold his glove up and put it in his pocket. I can see him now, strutting down to the bullpen and the fans cheering."

Carl Erskine once said that Labine would have made a great starter, but he preferred relieving. He liked the challenge. In the playoff for the 1951 pennant, Labine beat the Giants, 10–0, at the Polo Grounds. In the 1956 World Series, Labine beat the Yankees, 1–0, going ten innings. Clem was at the end of his career when he pitched in Los Angeles, but he was on the 1959 World Series champion Dodger team and then skipped to the staff of the 1960 World Champion Pittsburgh Pirates after a very brief stay in Detroit. After baseball, Labine returned to Rhode Island and became a designer for men's athletic wear and general manager for a sporting goods company. He died in 2007 at age eighty following brain surgery and a bout with pneumonia. He also was an instructor in the Dodgers' adult fantasy camp. Vin Scully once said, after the pitcher's death, that he had the "heart of a lion, the smarts of a wily fox and was very likable."

**17. Tim Crews, RP (1987–92), 11-13, 15 saves**. Tim Crews, who hails from Tampa, Florida, played six years in the Major Leagues, all with the Los Angeles Dodgers. He gets this high up because he pitched 423+ innings (sixth among all Dodger relievers) with an ERA of 3.44. His record was only 11-13, and he had 15 saves. Crews was drafted by the Milwaukee Brewers in 1980 but ended up going to the Dodgers. He signed with the Cleveland Indians but never pitched for them. He was killed in a boating accident on March 23, 1993. He was thirty-one years old. Cleveland reliever Steve Olin was also killed. These were the first deaths of Major Leaguers since Thurman Munson was killed in a plane crash in 1979.

**16. Ken Howell, RP (1984–88), 18-29, 31 saves**. Howell pitched 302 innings from 1984 to 1988 and finished 20-29. His overall ERA was 4.05, but he had good years in 1985 and 1986, saving 12 games each year. The only reason he ranks ahead of Labine is the fact that he had better years in Los Angeles. He was born in Detroit and was drafted by the Dodgers in 1982. He only pitched in the majors from 1984 to 1990—five years with L.A. and two with the Phillies. He has been the Dodgers' bullpen coach since 2008.

**15. Jim Gott, RP (1990–94), 19-22, 38 saves**. Gott pitched 339 1/3 innings with a 19-22 record. His ERA was a great 2.99. A native of San Marino, California, Gott was drafted in 1977 by the St. Louis Cardinals. He pitched five years for the Dodgers, from 1990 to 1994. Gott pitched fourteen years in the majors, posting an overall record of 56-74. His biggest year for the Dodgers was 1993 when he saved 25 games with an ERA of 2.32. Married with six children, Gott is pitching coach for the Arizona Angels minor-league team.

**14. Ed Roebuck, RP (1958–63), 22-10, 22 saves**. In 1955, at the age of twenty-three, Roebuck had 12 saves for the World Champion Brooklyn Dodgers. Ed pitched in Los Angeles from 1958 to 1963, earning 22 saves and a 22-10 record, good for an impressive .688 winning percentage, tied with Phil Regan for the best all-time among L.A. Dodgers relievers. He also had a lifetime ERA of 3.31. Ed came from East Millsboro, Pennsylvania, and signed with the Dodgers in 1955, becoming an important cog in their staff for eight years, and that's why he ranks this high. He was 10-2 in 1962 with 9 saves. Roebuck became a scout for the Dodgers, Braves, Reds, Pirates and Red Sox, retiring in 2004.

**13. Phil Regan, RP (1966–68), 22-10, 27 saves**. It's funny that two important relievers like Roebuck and Regan ended up with the same won-lost record. Regan only pitched 220+ innings for the Dodgers but was very important to their success from 1966 to 1968. He had 27 saves with a minuscule ERA of 2.28. He had two big years for the Dodgers, going 14-1 with 21 saves in 1966 and 12-5 with 25 saves in 1968. He pitched in two games in the 1966 World Series with an ERA of 0.00. Reagan went on to pitch thirteen seasons in the majors, going 96-81, including two good years with the Chicago Cubs. He was born in Michigan in 1937 and started playing for Detroit in 1960. Regan served many years as a pitching coach and manager in college, the minors and the majors.

**12. Mike Marshall, RP (1974–76), 28-29, 42 saves**. Marshall was known for pitching in a phenomenal 106 games in 1974 and 91 in 1973. He won the Cy Young Award in 1974, the first relief pitcher to do so. He was 14-11, with 31 saves in 1973 and 15-12 with 21 saves in 1974. His ERA was 2.66 in 1973 and 2.42 in 1974. He also pitched in ninety games for Minnesota in 1980. He ended up pitching for fourteen seasons, logging a

97-112 record and 188 saves. Born in Michigan, he was taken by Detroit in 1967 at age twenty-four.

Marshall has a PhD in kinesiology and teaches and advocates a pitching method he developed that he believes could eradicate pitching-arm injuries. Marshall says that in order to pitch, the arm has to externally rotate (hand lays back) before the ball accelerates. Traditionally, he says, the thrower often lifts his elbow before his hand. This leads to the ball coming up late and the arm to externally rotate late: "The elbow will be accelerated forward while the hand still goes backward, which creates enormous stress on the arm," he says. Of course, each pitcher has his own style and effectiveness, as well as a way of learning the sport and becoming successful in it.

**11. Steve Howe**, **LP (1980–83, 1985), 24-25, 59 saves**. Howe could have been a great pitcher for the Dodgers, but he got deeply involved in drugs. Born in Pontiac, Michigan, Howe was a star at the University of Michigan before being drafted by the Dodgers in 1980. A hard thrower, he immediately set a rookie record for saves (17) and was named Rookie of the Year—the third Dodger pitcher (Fernando Valenzuela and Rick Sutcliffe were the others) to be named in four years. He admitted to substance abuse and went on to be suspended for drug abuse seven times in his twelve-year career. It was too bad. He saved 59 games for the Dodgers in 327+ innings with a great 2.36 ERA. He pitched 7.1 innings in the 1988 World Series, recording a save. He signed with the Yankees in 1991 and had two good years before he became the second ballplayer to be banned from baseball for life. He was reinstated after an appeal and went on to have four more good years, including 1994, when he posted 15 saves and a miniscule ERA of 1.80. Steve later wrote a book about his frailties and tried to overcome his problems. He was killed in an auto accident in California in 2006 at the age of forty-eight. An autopsy reportedly showed that he had methamphetamine in his system.

**10. Takashi Saito, RP (2006–8), 12-7, 81 saves**. This guy never came to the Major Leagues until age thirty-six, but he has to be ranked this high because he was so effective. Saito only pitched three years for the Dodgers but had an incredible 81 saves in that time with a fantastic ERA of 1.95. His won-lost record was 12-7, and he only pitched 189+ innings. Born in Japan, he was a baseball all-star four times on the nation of islands, but he was plagued with injuries. After three years with the Dodgers, he spent his last three years with Boston, Atlanta and Milwaukee. He currently has a lifetime record of 21-15 and an ERA of 2.18. In December 2011, he signed a one-year deal with the Arizona Diamondbacks.

**9. Larry Sherry, RP (1958–63), 34-25, 39 saves**. Why in the world is Larry Sherry, who only had 34 wins and 39 saves, deserving of a top-ten rank on this list? One reason is that he pitched 503-plus innings, which makes him fourth among relievers. Another reason is that he had a great, great World Series in 1959. A third reason is that he was a consistently solid performer. Sherry's 1959 World Series performance was one of the greatest of all time. He played an important part in all four victories: he won 2 games and saved the other 2. He pitched 12+ innings with an ERA of 0.71. Born in Los Angeles, he was signed by the Brooklyn Dodgers out of Fairfax High School in 1953. He did not make his debut in the bigs until 1958, when he pitched 4+ innings with no decisions. But in 1959, he went 7-1 with a 2.19 ERA. He also had 3 saves and struck out 114 in 141 innings. He was 14-10 in 1960 and 7-3 in 1962. He pitched 503+ innings with the Dodgers, going 34-25 with an ERA of 3.48. He ended up pitching eleven seasons in the majors, going 53-44 with 82 saves, 39 with the Dodgers. Nobody will ever forget that 1959 World Series. Larry was a pitching coach after he retired. He died in 2006 at age seventy-one after a long battle with cancer.

**8. Tom Niedenfuer, RP (1981–87), 3-28, 75 saves**. Niedenfuer pitched seven years for the Dodgers, going 30-28. He struck out 339 guys in 438-plus innings. Niedenfuer deserves this lofty position because of 75 saves and a great ERA of 2.76. He signed with the Los Angeles Dodgers out of Washington State University in 1980 and started pitching for them in 1981. He appeared in two games in the 1981 World Series, posting an ERA of 0.00. His best years were 1983, when he went 8-3, and 1985, when he had 19 saves. He ended up pitching ten years in the majors, with stints with Baltimore, Seattle and St. Louis, finishing with a record of 36-46 and an ERA of 3.29. He married actress Judy Landers and last resided in Florida.

**7. Jonathan Broxton, RP (2005–2010), 25-20, 84 saves**. Broxton is a phenomenon. He may be the only three-hundred-pounder in the Major Leagues. The twenty-seven-year-old pitcher out of Augusta, Georgia, was signed out of high school by the Dodgers in 2002 and made his debut in 2005. Through 2011 he saved 84 ballgames. He has a won-lost mark of

25-20 and an ERA of 3.19 with 503 strikeouts in 392 innings. Broxton made his big-league debut against the St. Louis Cardinals on July 29, 2005. He struck out two and allowed one run. He played in fourteen games, striking out 22 batters in only 13 2/3 innings. He started the 2006 season in the minors but was quickly recalled. He became a setup man and only allowed a .159 batting average with runners in scoring position. From 2006 to 2010, he got a lot of work, appearing in 68, 83, 70, 73 and 64 games, respectively. He appeared in 83 games in 2007, the fourth most in franchise history. Broxton also recorded 96+ consecutive innings without allowing a home run, the longest streak in Los Angeles Dodgers history. He played in 2011, but a serious injury shut him down. He became a free agent in November 2011 and signed a one-year deal with Kansas City. He will be missed.

**6. Jeff Shaw, RP (1998–2001), 9-17, 129 saves**. It's hard to settle on the order of 4, 5, 6 relievers, but here goes. Pitching for the Dodgers in his last four years in the majors, Shaw saved a whopping total of 129 games, with an ERA of 3.37. He was only 9-17 in the won-lost column in that time, and he only pitched 234+ innings, but he made those innings memorable. A native of Ohio, he was drafted in 1986 out of the University of Rio Grande in Ohio. He started pitching for Cleveland in 1990. He also pitched for Montreal, the Chicago White Sox and Cincinnati, compiling 203 saves in twelve years. His save record with the Dodgers was 25, 34, 27 and 43, respectively—not chopped liver. He retired after the 2001 season, when he saved 43 games. He was thirty-four.

**5. Todd Worrell, RP (1993–97), 17-19, 127 saves**. Worrell saved 2 fewer games for the Dodgers than Jeff Shaw, but he had a more impressive mound presence. Worrell won 17 and lost 19 with a 3.93 ERA. He struck out more than Shaw, but he also walked considerably more, eighty to Shaw's fifty-six. Worrell, who was born in Arcadia, California, joined the St. Louis Cardinals in 1985 and recorded 129 saves in six years. But he tore his rotator cuff and missed the 1990 and 1991 seasons. He came back in 1992 with St. Louis but, at the end of the year, signed with the Dodgers as a free agent. He finally returned to his old form in 1995 and proceeded to save 32, 44 and 35 games in his final three years, making two All-Star Game appearances as a Dodger. Worrell is also ranked forty-first all-time in games finished with 456. At his best, he was great. Todd has three sons who play ball and is currently a college pitching coach.

**4. Jay Howell, RP (1988–92), 22-19, 129 saves**. Jay Howell is a product of Fairfield High School and the University of Colorado (my alma mater), both in Boulder. He joined the Cincinnati Reds in 1980, came to the Dodgers in 1988 and proceeded to save 85 games in five years. Howell pitched 307+ innings, and his great ERA (2.07) and his 22 victories land him in this spot. He was infamous for getting suspended for two games in the third game of that year's National League playoffs against the New York Mets for having pine tar in his glove. He ended up pitching fifteen years in the majors with Cincinnati, the Chicago Cubs, New York Yankees, Oakland, Atlanta and Texas. He saved 155 games, which puts him fifty-sixth on the all-time list. Howell coached from 1996 through 2005 at Cal State Northridge.

**3. Eric Gagne, RP (1999–2006), 25-21, 161 saves**. Why is a guy with 161 saves relegated to third on this all-time list? Well, Gagne did appear in 545+ innings, quite a lot, but not compared to the two top relievers. Gagne was 25-21 and had 629 strikeouts. He also logged only 182 walks. At his best, he was lights-out, virtually unhittable. Born in Montreal, he grew up in the small town of Mascouche, Quebec. He spoke only French when he went to study at Seminole Junior College in Seminole, Oklahoma. He was drafted by the Chicago White Sox in 1994 but signed with the Dodgers as a free agent in 1995. He didn't make the big club until 1999 at age twenty-three. He struggled as a starter, and the Dodgers converted him to a reliever. In 2002, he had 52 saves, and in 2003, he had 55 saves and an ERA of 1.20 and won the Cy Young Award. He and Ferguson Jenkins are the only Canadians to win the Cy Young Award. Between August 26, 2002, and July 5, 2004, he saved 84 straight games, a record. He had 45 saves in 2004, but then injuries struck and he had elbow surgery in 2005 and back surgery in 2006. He signed with Texas in 2007 and saved 16 games and then 8 with Milwaukee in 2008. Then he retired, never the same pitcher after his injuries. Many people thought the Dodgers overpitched him.

**2. Ron Perranowski, LP (1961–67), 54-41, 101 saves**. Perranowski and Jim Brewer are the two best L.A. Dodgers relievers, and one had to be selected over the other. In 1963, "Perry" was 16-3, tied for third for most all-time wins for a reliever in a year, with 21 saves. Perranowski saved 101 games and went 52-41 in seven years. His ERA was 2.56, which ranks number one among Dodgers relievers who pitched more than 400 innings. Perranowski struck out 461 in 766-plus innings. Born in 1936 in Paterson, New Jersey, Ron attended Michigan State University, where he was a teammate of Dick Radatz, who also was a standout reliever in the 1960s. Perry was signed by the Chicago Cubs in 1958 and was traded to the Dodgers in 1960 for Don Zimmer. Perry had a nice seven years for the Dodgers, even though his biggest year was the World Series–winning year of 1963, when he had but 1 save. He was also on the blue teams that won the World Series in 1965 and lost it to Baltimore in 1966. Besides the Dodgers, Ron pitched with Minnesota, Detroit and California, saving another 78 games. His lifetime ERA was 2.79, pretty spectacular. Perranowski spent fourteen years as the Dodgers' pitching coach and has been associated with the Giants since 1985 and since 2000 as assistant to General Manager Brian Sabean.

**1. Jim Brewer, LP (1964–75), 61-51, 125 saves**. Brewer and Perranoski are virtually tied on paper, but Brewer just gets the no. 1 spot. He recorded 125 saves (24 more than Ron), a record of 61-51 and a miniscule ERA of 2.62. He also pitched 786-plus innings. He didn't come to the Dodgers until 1964, so he was in only two World Series. But he pitched eleven seasons for the Dodgers, with his best year probably being 1968, when he went 8-3 and saved 14 games. He saved, 14, 20, 24, 22, 17 and 20 games, respectively, from 1968 through 1973. He pitched in three World Series and was on the winning team in 1965. Brewer also pitched for the Chicago Cubs and California Angels. He finished with 132 saves in seventeen seasons with an ERA of 3.07.

Brewer, from Broken Arrow, Oklahoma, came up with the Chicago Cubs in 1960. He is infamous for a fight with Billy Martin in 1960 when he was with the Cubs and Martin was with Cincinnati. Billy thought he got too close with a brush-back pitch. Martin threw his bat at Jim, who picked it up to hand it back. Then the notoriously volatile Martin slugged him, breaking his cheekbone. Brewer was out of action for two months. Martin was suspended for five days, and the Cubs sued him for $1 million for the loss of Brewer's services. Brewer also sued him and collected $10,000. Martin sarcastically cracked, "How do they want it? Cash or check?"

THE 25 GREATEST LOS ANGELES DODGER RELIEF PITCHERS

| Rank | Years Played | Name | Total Innings | Saves per Year | W-L | ERA (ER) | Saves | SO | BB | W-L % |
|---|---|---|---|---|---|---|---|---|---|---|
| 1. | 1964–75 | Jim Brewer | 822+ | 10.4 | 61-51 | 2.62 (239) | 125 | 672 | 298 | .545 |
| 2. | 1961–67 | Ron Perranoski | 766+ | 12,6 | 54-41 | 2.56 (218) | 101 | 461 | 290 | .568 |
| 3. | 1999–2006 | Eric Gagne | 545+ | 20.1 | 25-21 | 3.27 (198) | 161 | 629 | 182 | .543 |
| 4. | 1988–92 | Jay Howell | 308+ | 17 | 22-19 | 2.07 (71) | 129 | 260 | 92 | .537 |
| 5. | 1993–97 | Todd Worrell | 268 | 25.4 | 17-19 | 3.93 (117) | 127 | 263 | 80 | .472 |
| 6. | 1998–2001 | Jeff Shaw | 235+ | 32.3 | 9-17 | 3.37 (88) | 129 | 166 | 56 | .346 |
| 7. | 2005–2011 | Jon Broxton | 392 | 12 | 25-20 | 3.19 (139) | 84 | 503 | 163 | .555 |
| 8. | 1981–87 | Tom Niedenfuer | 441 | 10.7 | 30-28 | 2.76 (135) | 64 | 350 | 75 | .517 |
| 9. | 1958–63 | Larry Sherry | 505+ | 6.5 | 34-25 | 3.48 (195) | 39 | 385 | 239 | .576 |

# Seven Decades of Diamond Dominance

| | | | | | | | | | | | |
|---|---|---|---|---|---|---|---|---|---|---|---|
| 10. | 2006–8 | Takashi Saito | 189+ | 27 | 12-7 | 1.95 (41) | 81 | 245 | 52 | .632 |
| 11. | 1984–85 | Steve Howe | 327+ | 11.8 | 24-25 | 2.36 (86) | 59 | 213 | 74 | .490 |
| 12. | 1974–76 | Mike Marshall | 380+ | 14 | 28-29 | 3.01 (127) | 42 | 246 | 120 | .491 |
| 13. | 1966–68 | Phil Regan | 220+ | 9 | 22-10 | 2.28 (56) | 27 | 148 | 67 | .688 |
| 14. | 1958–63 | Ed Roebuck | 321 | 4.4 | 22-10 | 3.31 (118) | 22 | 209 | 130 | .688 |
| 15. | 1990–94 | Jim Gott | 340 | 7.6 | 19-22 | 2.99 (113) | 38 | 288 | 144 | .463 |
| 16. | 1984–88 | Ken Howell | 302+ | 6.2 | 18-29 | 4.04 (136) | 31 | 315 | 140 | .383 |
| 17. | 1987–92 | Tim Crews | 423+ | 2.5 | 11-13 | 3.44 (162) | 15 | 293 | 110 | .458 |
| 18. | 1958–60 | Clem Labine | 205.+ | 8 | 11-17 | 4.21 (96) | 24 | 95 | 66 | .393 |
| 19. | 1978–82 | Terry Forster | 207 | 5.4 | 11-13 | 3.48 (80) | 27 | 125 | 84 | .458 |

| Rank | Years Played | Name | Total Innings | Saves per Year | W-L | ERA (ER) | Saves | SO | BB | W-L % |
|---|---|---|---|---|---|---|---|---|---|---|
| 20. | 1991–94 | Roger McDowell | 235+ | 5.8 | 17-19 | 3.48 (91) | 23 | 128 | 110 | .472 |
| 21. | 1981–85 | Bobby Castillo | 286+ | 3.6 | 15-16 | 3.90 (124) | 18 | 157 | 117 | .483 |
| 22. | 1996–98 | Scott Radinsky | 176+ | 5.7 | 16-8 | 2.66 (52) | 17 | 137 | 58 | .666 |
| 23. | 2005–2010 | Hong Chi Kuo | 292+ | 1.9 | 13-17 | 3.73 (121) | 13 | 345 | 127 | .433 |
| 24. | 1989–91 | John Wetteland | 154+ | 0.3 | 8-12 | 3.84 (66) | 1 | 141 | 54 | .400 |
| 25. | 2004–8 | Yhency Brazoban | 115 | 4.2 | 10-12 | 4.70 (60) | 21 | 100 | 55 | .455 |

# The Best of Dodger Starting and Relief Pitchers

## STARTING

### MOST STRIKEOUTS

| | | |
|---|---|---|
| 1. | Don Sutton | 2,696 |
| 2. | Don Drysdale | 2,383 |
| 3. | Sandy Koufax | 2,214 |
| 4. | Fernando Valenzuela | 1,759 |
| 5. | Orel Hershiser | 1,456 |
| 6. | Ramon Martinez | 1,314 |
| 7. | Bob Welch | 1,292 |
| 8. | Chan Ho Park | 1,177 |
| 9. | Claude Osteen | 1,162 |
| 10. | Burt Hooton | 1,042 |

## Most Strikeouts Per 9 Innings

| | | |
|---|---|---|
| 1. | Antonio Osuna | 9.6 |
| 2. | Sandy Koufax | 9.4 |
| 3. | Clayton Kershaw | 9.3 |
| 4. | Hideo Nomo | 8.8 |
| 5. | Chan HoPark | 8.3 |
| 6. | Darren Dreifort | 8.3 |
| 7. | Kevin Brown | 8.1 |
| 8. | Kazuhisa Ishii | 7.2 |
| 8. | Randy Wolf | 7.2 |
| 10. | Tim Belcher | 7.1 |

## Best ERA Lifetime

| | | |
|---|---|---|
| 1. | Sandy Koufax | 2.64 |
| 2. | Andy Messersmith | 2.67 |
| 3. | Guillermo Mota | 2.79 |
| 4. | Kevin Brown | 2.83 |
| 5. | Clayton Kershaw | 2.87 |
| 6. | Alejandro Pena | 2.92 |
| 7. | Tommy John | 2.97 |
| 8. | Don Drysdale | 2.98 |
| 9. | Tim Belcher | 2.99 |
| 10. | Bill Singer | 3.03 |

## Least Walks per 9 Innings

| | | |
|---|---|---|
| 1. | Odalis Perez | 2.0 |
| 2. | Claude Osteen | 2.1 |
| 2. | Hiroki Kuroda | 2.1 |
| 2. | Jerry Reuss | 2.1 |
| 5. | Don Drysdale | 2.2 |
| 5. | Tommy John | 2.2 |

| 7. | Mike Morgan | 2.3 |
|----|-------------|-----|
| 7. | Derek Lowe | 2.3 |
| 7. | Don Stuton | 2.3 |
| 10. | Ishmael Valdez | 2.5 |

## BEST WON-LOST PERCENTAGE

| 1. | Tommy John | .674 |
|----|------------|------|
| 2. | Sandy Koufax | .670 |
| 3. | Kevin Brown | .644 |
| 4. | Rick Rhoden | .636 |
| 5. | Roger Craig | .634 |
| 6. | Andy Messersmith | .618 |
| 7. | Ramon Martinez | .615 |
| 8. | Matt Herges | .606 |
| 9. | Randy Wolf | .606 |
| 10. | Chan Ho Park | .592 |

## MOST INNINGS PITCHED

| 1. | Don Sutton | 3,816 |
|----|------------|-------|
| 2. | Don Drysdale | 3,112 |
| 3. | Claude Osteen | 2,397 |
| 4. | Fernando Valenzuela | 2,348 |
| 5. | Orel Hershiser | 2,180 |
| 6. | Sandy Koufax | 2,119 |
| 7. | Burt Hooton | 1,861 |
| 8. | Bob Welch | 1,820 |
| 9. | Ramon Martinez | 1,731 |
| 10. | Johnny Podres | 1,407 |

# Relief

## Best ERA Lifetime

| | | |
|---|---|---|
| 1. | Takashi Saito | 1.95 |
| 2. | Jay Howell | 2.07 |
| 3. | Phil Regan | 2.28. |
| 4. | Steve Howe | 2.36. |
| 5. | Ron Perranosk | 2.56. |
| 6. | Jim Brewer | 2.61 |
| 7. | Scott Radinsky | 2.66. |
| 8. | Tom eNiedenfuer | 2.76 |
| 9. | Jim Gott | 2.99 |
| 10. | Mike Marshall | 3.01 |

## Most Saves

| | | |
|---|---|---|
| 1. | Eric Gagne | 161 |
| 2. | Jay Howell | 129 |
| 2. | Jeff Shaw | 129 |
| 4. | Todd Worrell | 127 |
| 5. | Jim Brewer | 125 |
| 6. | Ron Perranoski | 101 |
| 7. | Jonathan Broxton | 84 |
| 8. | Takashi Saito | 81 |
| 9. | Tom Niedenfurer | 75 |
| 10. | Larry Sherry | 39 |

## Most Innings

| | | |
|---|---|---|
| 1. | Jim Brewer | 822 |
| 2. | Ron Perranoski | 766 |
| 3. | Eric Gagne | 545 |
| 4. | Larry Sherry | 505 |
| 5. | Tom Niedenfurer | 441 |

| 6. | Tim Crews | 423 |
|----|-----------|-----|
| 7. | Jonathan Broxton | 392 |
| 8. | Mike Marshall | 380 |
| 9. | Jim Gott | 340 |
| 10. | Steve Howe | 327 |

## LOS ANGELES DODGERS TEAM ERA

| 1958 | 4.47 |
|------|------|
| 1959 | 3.79 |
| 1960 | 3.40 |
| 1961 | 4.04 |
| 1962 | 3.62 |
| 1963 | 2.85 |
| 1964 | 2.95 |
| 1965 | 2.81 |
| 1966 | 2.62 |
| 1967 | 3.21 |
| 1968 | 2.69 |
| 1969 | 3.08 |
| 1970 | 3.82 |
| 1971 | 3.23 |
| 1972 | 2.78 |
| 1973 | 3.00 |
| 1974 | 2.97 |
| 1975 | 2.92 |
| 1976 | 3.02 |
| 1977 | 3.22 |
| 1978 | 3.12 |
| 1979 | 3.83 |
| 1980 | 3.25 |
| 1981 | 3.01 |
| 1982 | 3.26 |
| 1983 | 3.10 |

| | |
|---|---|
| 1984 | 3.17 |
| 1985 | 2.96 |
| 1986 | 3.76 |
| 1987 | 3.72 |
| 1988 | 2.96 |
| 1989 | 2.95 |
| 1990 | 3.72 |
| 1991 | 3.06 |
| 1992 | 3.41 |
| 1993 | 3.50 |
| 1994 | 4.14 |
| 1995 | 3.66 |
| 1996 | 3.46 |
| 1997 | 3.62 |
| 1998 | 3.81 |
| 1999 | 4.45 |
| 2000 | 4.10 |
| 2001 | 4.25 |
| 2002 | 3.69 |
| 2003 | 3.16 |
| 2004 | 4.01 |
| 2005 | 4.38 |
| 2006 | 4.23 |
| 2007 | 4.20 |
| 2008 | 3.68 |
| 2009 | 3.41 |
| 2010 | 4.01 |
| 2011 | 3.54 |

# Bibliography

*The Baseball Encyclopedia*. New York: MacMillan, 1976.

Delsohn, Steve. *True Blue*. New York: Harper, 2001.

Drysdale, Don, with Bob Verdi. *Once a Bum, Always a Dodger*. New York: St. Martin's Press, 1990.

Gruver, Edward. *Koufax*. Dallas, TX: Taylor Publishing Company, 2000.

Hershiser, Orel, with Jerry B. Jenkins. *Out of the Blue*. Brentwood, TN: Wolgemuth & Hyatt, 1989.

Koufax, Sandy, with Ed Linn. *Koufax*. New York: Viking Press, 1966.

Langill, Mark. *Game of My Life: Dodgers*. Champaign, IL: Sports Publishing, LLC, 2007.

Leavy, Jane. *Sandy Koufax: A Lefty's Legacy*. New York: HarperCollins, 2002.

Morgan, Joe, and David Falkner. *Joe Morgan: A Life in Baseball*. New York: W.R. Norton & Company, 1993.

Nathan, David H. *The McFarland Baseball Quotations Dictionary*. Jefferson, NC: McFarland & Company, Inc., 2000.

Palmer, Pete, and Gary Gillette, eds. *The 2005 ESPN Baseball Encyclopedia*. New York: Sterling, 2005.

Smith, Curt. *Storied Stadiums*. New York: Carroll & Graf, 2001.

Snider, Duke, with Bill Gilbert. *The Duke of Flatbush*. New York: Kensington, 1988.

Thorne, John, Pete Palmer, et al. *Total Baseball.* 6th ed. New York: Total Sports, 1999.

Vecsey, George. *Stan Musical: An American Life.* New York: Ballantine Books, 2011.

# REFERENCE WEBSITES

Baseball-Almanac.com.

Baseball-Reference.com.

# About the Author

D on Lechman, a native of Colorado, worked as a reporter, critic and editor for the newspaper industry from 1960 to 2005. A graduate of the University of Colorado in journalism and a dedicated Buff, his columns appear regularly in the *Daily Breeze* newspaper in Torrance, California. You can also read him at donlechman.blogspot. com. Besides being a devoted fan of baseball, football and basketball, he enjoys writing, reading, traveling, playing the guitar, watching movies, listening to music, playing basketball, working out and spending time with his two grandchildren. He teaches writing at Los Angeles Harbor College in Wilmington. He has been married to artist Pat for thirty-eight years and has two children, Laura and David.

Visit us at
www.historypress.net